LAXMI PANDA

The Story of Netaji's Youngest Spy

Savie Karnel is the author of the critically acclaimed children's book, *The Nameless God*. Voted the most popular children's book on Amazon India in 2021, it was also shortlisted for the Bangalore Literature Festival Book Prize that same year. Notably, it was the only children's book shortlisted for the MAMI Film Festival's Words to Screen Options Market in 2023.

Savie grew up in the coastal town of Karwar and began her career as a journalist, reporting for *The New Indian Express*, *Mid-Day* and *Talk Magazine* in Bangalore. Now a children's author, she still finds inspiration in travel and the stories of those she meets. When she's not writing or dreaming up plots, Savie enjoys exploring new places and listening to stories from people she meets. She lives in Kolkata with her husband, son and two indie dogs.

For all the unknown soldiers of the Forgotten Army

Published by Red Panda, an imprint of Westland Books, a division of Nasadiya Technologies Private Limited, in 2024

No. 269/2B, First Floor, 'Irai Arul', Vimalraj Street, Nethaji Nagar, Alapakkam Main Road, Maduravoyal, Chennai 600095

ISBN: 9789360456788

10 9 8 7 6 5 4 3 2

Book typeset by New Media Line Creations, New Delhi

Printed at Thomson Press (India) Ltd

SAVIE KARNEL

LAXMI PANDA

THE STORY OF NETAJI'S YOUNGEST SPY

RED PANDA

AUTHOR'S NOTE

I vividly remember my first conversation with INA warrior Laxmi Panda. Her first words on the phone, 'Jai Hind!' gave me goosebumps. Instinctively, I straightened my back in attention. Such was the intensity and enthusiasm with which she uttered the salutation. It had been over 60 years since the Indian National Army was disbanded, and Laxmi was in her late 70s. Yet, she continued to greet with the same loud 'Jai Hind' that she must have learned during her training at the Rani of Jhansi Regiment. She had a poster of Netaji Subhas Chandra Bose on the wall of her hut and saluted it religiously.

Summoning her strength, Laxmi Panda narrated her experiences in the INA. 'I sat outside the camp gate for three days to meet Netaji and join the INA,' she said proudly, recalling that he named her Indira. When asked about her duties in the INA, she initially spoke of housekeeping and kitchen tasks before revealing, 'We would catch frogs and enter British camps to sell frog meat to the officers. We would then collect information from the camps and pass it on to the INA.' She was a spy! But she recounted it casually, beaming with pride when she revealed that she was never caught. 'There is no bravery in getting caught and going to jail. A smart soldier never gets caught by the enemy,' she said. True to her belief, she was never caught by the British and managed to evade arrest when confronted.

Born in Burma, Laxmi was ready to die for the motherland she had never seen until years later. She lost her parents in the bombings by the Allied Forces during World War II, survived with her younger brother Nakul and resolved to return to the motherland, which she knew only through her parents' stories. She also recalled the scarcity of food and surviving on boiled leaves, evading aerial attacks by the Allied Forces during the INA's retreat after its failure in the Imphal Campaign. Laxmi and other members of the Jhansi of Rani Regiment trekked for 26 days through the jungles of Burma to Bangkok before their journey to Singapore.

After the news of Netaji's death broke out, the INA was disbanded, and she made her way back to Burma. Though it was the only home she had known, she found no family there. She had lost her younger brother Nakul during the war and did not know his whereabouts. She then took a tramp boat to Chittagong. When confronted by the British, she threw away her uniform and other signs of the identity of the INA into the sea. Along with a few other INA soldiers, she reached Orissa.

Later, in 1951, she married a fellow INA soldier, Khogeswar Panda, and changed her last name from Rath to Panda. Since this book tells the story of Laxmi when she was unmarried in the INA, we refer to her by her maiden name, Laxmi Rath, not Laxmi Panda, as she is popularly known. While she was a soldier, she was called Indira to avoid confusion with the commander of the Rani of Jhansi Regiment, the famous Captain Lakshmi Sehgal, referred to by her maiden name, Captain Lakshmi Swaminathan.

When I first met her grandson, Probin Raj Patro, in 2008 in Bangalore, Laxmi was working as a domestic worker in Jeypore, Orissa, trying to make ends meet. Probin had been visiting all newspaper offices to draw attention to his freedom-fighter grandmother's plight. He approached me at the newspaper office where I worked as a reporter. He was trying to help his maternal grandmother, Laxmi Panda, get her due recognition from the union government and secure the freedom fighter's pension, allowing her to lead a dignified retired life.

With help from researcher and historian Anil Dhir, Laxmi could fulfil her lifelong dream of marching to Delhi. Her INA dream of 'Chalo Dilli!' was realised when the then-President Pratibha Patil invited her to Rashtrapati Bhavan. Laxmi was conferred with the Rashtiya Swatantrata Samman, a recognition for freedom fighters and a pension was granted. This honour came a little too late. A few days after the announcement, Laxmi breathed her last on October 7, 2008.

My heart sank when Probin called me with the news of Laxmi's demise. Life had been unfair to Laxmi Panda. She was a warrior and had valiantly fought various battles in life. Perhaps the most glorious years of her life were the couple of years she spent in the Rani of Jhansi Regiment. I felt this part of her life had to be celebrated, and her stories of courage had to be told. She deserved to be celebrated as a spy, a warrior and a patriot. I never stopped thinking about her. I decided that one day, I would tell the story of a young and brave child spy, Laxmi Indira Rath.

I began work on writing young Laxmi's story in 2022, 14 years after my encounter with her. By then, people's memories had faded. Her grandchildren didn't remember the exact details. In her last years, all the focus of journalists and her well-wishers was on her poverty. With the intention of helping her, everyone had highlighted her current state and forgotten to unearth her valiant past.

She is remembered as a child spy of Netaji's army; but incidents, routes, the missions she undertook, and specifics were lost. I didn't want these impediments to deter my resolve to tell her story. Her journey could not be lost because we failed to document it.

I read up on the INA, the Rani of Jhansi Regiment, their daily routine, the military campaigns they undertook, and the documented incidents. I wove Laxmi's adventures with my imagination around these incidents and her revelations. This book tells a fictionalised account of the child spy. This is my tribute to Laxmi Indira and the many unknown soldiers of Azad Hind Fauj.

Chapter 1

HIDE-AND-SEEK

My favourite game in the whole wide world is hide-and-seek, or as my brother and I call it, Koo-kui. That's the sound the seeker makes after counting to ten. It goes like this: 'One, two, three, four … ten! Ready or not, here I come,' followed by a high-pitched 'Koooooo … kui!' That's the signal for all the hiders to settle down where they are and stop looking for safer spots. It's supposed to sound like the cry of a bird, perhaps like the hornbills who fly through the jungles of Burma. Instead, we end up sounding like the crows in a Rangoon bazaar.

'Lakhmi! Oooo … Lakhmi! Come and help me with the chores and then take your brother outside to play luchakali so I can cook in peace,' Ma used to say in Oriya.

'Why should I be the only one doing chores? Why shouldn't he help too?' I argued one day.

'You're almost thirteen now. You need to learn,' she said. When she noticed my expression, she added, 'Nakul is young. You know he'll only create a mess if I ask him to help.'

I had to agree with her on this. You know how younger siblings can be. You have to give them whatever they want and go along with everything they say. You have to play with them—and only the games they like, or else they cry and stomp their feet. They're like mini devils with their tantrums. 'The older sibling always suffers,' I'd tell Nakul.

'No way,' he'd quickly reply. 'It's us younger ones who have a hard time. Everyone keeps scolding and correcting me. You and the grown-ups boss me around. I have to do whatever you say and can't even answer back. You think I'm a baby but I'm almost as old as you—ten or eleven, I think.'

'I think, huh,' I would sneer. The truth is that neither of us knows our exact age. We know we were born in the 1930s, but not the exact year. When we asked Ma, she said, 'We moved here after the earthquake. Nakul, you were born around Jagannath Rath Yatra and Lakhmi, you were born around Lakhmi Puja. It rained so much both those years.'

'Rained where, Ma?' I asked.

'Here, in Burma. You were both born in Burma.'

'Did it rain a lot in India too?'

'I don't know. I haven't been there since I married your Baba and came here to lay railway lines for the gora sahebs.' The British had brought many labourers from India to help construct the railways in Burma. Ma–Baba were among them.

Whenever we spoke of India, Ma's eyes would drift westwards. 'I hope the gora sahebs finish the railways here soon. Then we can all return to our villages and families,' she'd say.

'Tell us more about Hind, Ma,' Nakul and I would prod.

Ma would drop all her chores and tell us how she'd wait for the village fair all year long and how much she missed the food. Though she cooked dalma and rice for us, when we would sit down to eat, she would say, 'Nah, nah. It's not the same. The bhaat and dal here are different from those in my village. The quality of crops depends on the soil too. The soil back home gives a unique fragrance and taste to the rice and dal grown there. It's magical. And the chhena poda—it just melts in your mouth.'

During one of these conversations, Nakul couldn't help but tease Ma: 'So you mean the cows there give magical milk that makes chhena poda different?'

Ma's expression grew serious. 'Yes, yes. The milk is also different. I told you the soil there is special.'

'But cows don't eat soil, Ma.'

'They eat grass, and that grows in soil. The grass there is different from here, and so the milk is special.'

Nakul looked worried. 'But, Ma, if the grass and soil make the cows there special, what about us? Maybe we're not as special as the children in Hind. Maybe we're just ordinary children.'

'No child is ordinary,' Ma said. 'Every child has starlight within them. The stars you were born under, your nakshatra, shine through you and guide you. As we grow older, we start ignoring that light, and our wrong choices and deeds dim that light.'

'Wouldn't it have been better to be born in Bharat?,' asked Lakhmi.

'There's a reason for everything, so I'm sure there's a reason you two were born in Burma. We may not know what it is right now, but there's always a greater plan,' Ma said. 'Not being born in the land of our ancestors, or living away from it, doesn't mean we love our motherland any less. It's just circumstances that have brought us here. Someday soon, we'll return home.'

These were foolish hopes. The British bosses had all gone into hiding. Soon after the Japanese first bombed Burma, on a Christmas Eve, it was the last time we saw the gora sahebs. The memsaheb who complained about 'the bloodthirsty mosquitoes and the hellish heat' throughout the year, except during winter, had been in a good mood a few days before the attack. 'Merry Christmas!' she greeted all of us with a broad smile. She had taught us kids English and was the only one, other than my parents, who pronounced my name in the Oriya way: 'Lakhmi'. Ma said that was because 'sh' was a tongue twister for Memsaheb. She couldn't say Laxmi without making us all chuckle. 'Is it Lucky-is-me? Lucky-is-she-me? Luckyish-me?'

My mother, who always pushed me to speak up, prodded, 'Lakhmi, help memsaheb with your name.'

'What did you call her?' asked memsaheb.

'In Oriya, we say Lakhmi. But her name is Laxmi. Laxmi Rath,' Ma muttered, scared that Memsaheb might think we lied to make her tongue twist.

'Luck-me. Lakhmi is perfect. Easy,' she said and stuck to it.

They were nice people. Ma said the gora saheb was only doing his job, just like Baba was doing his. But some could be nasty, like the saheb's superior. Whenever he visited, he'd look down his big nose at us and twitch it so much that the hair in his nostrils would stick out. He didn't say anything, but you could tell he thought we were filthy. The real evil firangis, way worse than him, were the ones in palaces who made the rules that suited the British government.

On Christmas Eve, we sat around a bonfire with our neighbours. I liked facing away from the fire to warm my back, holding my palms open behind me to feel the heat. 'Get away from there. Don't stand so close,' Ma cautioned.

'Your back could get burnt from the sparks flying off the wood. But if you're facing the fire, you can dodge them,' my friend Mariamma said. She whistled, imitating the sparks, and pretended to dodge them. 'Like this! Swing like this.'

'What if a spark hits your eye?' I asked.

'Then shut it,' she said. She playfully splashed some water on my face. 'See, you immediately closed your eyes. That's how it works with sparks too.'

I loved her mother's idlis and chutney, but not in winter. They would turn out hard, not fluffy like in other seasons. 'The batter doesn't ferment well in the cold,' Mariamma explained. But that evening, on Christmas Eve, they were perfect despite the chill.

Mariamma chuckled when she saw my excitement. Then she told me the secret to making fluffy idlis in winter: 'Amma kept the utensil with the batter in warm water. She kept changing the water whenever it cooled off, over and over again. She woke up so many times throughout the night just for that. She kept it under the bright sun this morning, and then it was magic. The batter rose and began to spill over—foo, foo, foo—and before it could overflow ... tak! Amma scooped it up and poured it into the moulds.'

'Oh! Is this my mould? The one I made?' Nakul asked.

'No, this one. This shapeless idli is from your mould. The idlis you made didn't hold together,' Mariamma handed him an idli shaped like a squashed mango.

'I don't want this. I'll take one from my sister's mould,' he said.

The previous day, Mariamma, Nakul and I had climbed a jackfruit tree and plucked its leaves. We had then woven them into moulds, pinning them in place with tiny twigs. We'd do this every time Mariamma's amma wanted to make idlis. Once the idlis were steamed in them, the leaf moulds would be thrown away. 'There's no point gathering things when we're always on the move. Maybe someday, we'll settle down and set up a home, and we won't have to move again. Then I'll buy more utensils,' Mariamma's amma often said.

That evening, while we chatted and ate around the fire, a sound like thunder rumbled through the sky. 'What was that?' I asked.

'Maybe it's going to rain,' said Mariamma, chomping on her idli dipped in chicken curry.

'Rain in December isn't unusual in these parts,' added her amma.

'I like to say there are just two seasons here: the monsoon and winter. Now, I'll have to say that it just rains here throughout the year,' Ma said.

'But look, Ma, there are no clouds,' Nakul said, pointing to the sky.

Tension hung in the air. When things didn't seem right, Ma would hurry us back to the only place we felt safe—our house. The fire was put out and everyone quickly left, wondering what the sound could be.

That night, I held Ma tightly, frightened by the thundering sounds that came without lightning or clouds. It felt like the day we played at the edge of the forest. We had heard a roar, or something like a roar, but didn't see anything. No pug marks, no beast. That felt scarier than if we had spotted a leopard or a bear because we could have simply run away from it. Seeing nothing only worried us. Was it an animal? A monster? A ghost? Ma said that ghosts are scarier than animals because we cannot see them and don't know how they can hurt us. Our imagination makes them seem even more dreadful. Mariamma said that though animals can attack us, ghosts can possess us, and those scars last much longer. These sounds were like that, unseen yet frightening, leaving scars that would last.

The next morning, the supplies that were to come from Rangoon for the Christmas party at Saheb's bungalow didn't arrive. Memsaheb had grown restless and was panicking. Ma had gone early that day to finish the chores in Memsaheb's kitchen and waited for the orders. Instead, she saw Memsaheb pacing up and down the parlour, sweating and cracking her knuckles. Later that day, we heard the news: Rangoon had been bombed. The Japanese had attacked Burma, a British territory. The sounds we had heard the previous night were air raids. Burma was being bombed by Japanese planes.

Our evenings were never the same after that. No more bonfires with our neighbours. No more sharing meals while sitting around the fire for warmth. We were ordered not to light any fires so airplanes couldn't spot our houses at night. The nights had turned darker and colder.

The officers said that railway lines are usually the first to be destroyed during attacks to stop transportation and communication. We had to be extra cautious. The windows of the gora saheb's bungalow were painted black. The only lights that remained were that of the glow-worms hopping over the grass.

News of more air strikes across Burma kept trickling in. The bombings went on for months. Perhaps it was because we were in the interiors, far away from the capital, Rangoon, and almost in a forest that no bombs fell on our houses. We heard the Japanese Imperial Army was advancing into Burma and occupying different areas. The railway line construction work stopped. There were whispers that very soon, the Japanese Imperial Army would take over Burma and free it of the British.

Baba didn't believe it. 'The British call England "the empire on which the sun never sets". Their territories extend all over the world. I don't think the Japanese emperor can defeat the British,' he said to Bidya's father.

'You know, I often hear the goras talk,' Bidya's father said. 'I've heard that the Japanese call their home "the land of the rising sun". It's like a war between the sun that never sets and the sun that's rising.'

One day, when Mariamma's mother went to the saheb's house to work, she found no one there. The house was abandoned. She saw Bidya's mother return from the other gora saheb's house that she worked in. 'No one's there. No one in the house,' she told Ma. The two went around enquiring and found the British houses abandoned. All the British officers had left.

'They've all gone. There's no one left. No one,' she announced, breathless from running back to our neighbourhood.

'How can they just leave us?' asked Bidya's mother, who had come all the way from Nepal. 'Where have they gone?'

'I'd overheard Memsaheb saying something about them returning to India,' admitted Mariamma's amma. 'But I thought they meant sometime in the future, not now.

Didn't we all plan to return to our homes in India with them one day?'

'Yes, we thought they would arrange our return, the same way they brought us here on ships,' said Ma.

'They should have,' said Bidya's mother. 'They cannot abandon us like this in a foreign forest.'

All the families of the railway workers were panicked. Ma–Baba were worried about not receiving wages any more. Where would our next meal come from? How long could we survive on just their savings? Would they get another job? Suddenly, Burma, the country I was born in, the only country I had known all my life, didn't seem like home. For the first time, I realised that my parents and all my neighbours were foreigners, left behind by the British amidst a war, their war. Like the jackfruit leaf moulds used to make idlis, we had been thrown away.

Chapter 2

ESCAPE THROUGH DEATH VALLEY

As the weeks passed, the bombings continued and people began leaving. The foreigners in Burma were returning home.

One morning, Bidya came to me with her favourite doll, the one she'd sewn from old rags. 'Can you take care of her?' she asked, handing her over to me. Bidya had had the blue-white doll with her for a couple of years. Her body was made from an old white saree with blue flower prints. I had never liked the doll much because, over time, she had turned light brown and looked like a limp, tattooed body. She wasn't exactly sweet looking. Bidya had given her two charcoal eyes, which only made her look scarier. But Bidya loved her and took her with her everywhere. I was surprised that she was handing her over to me, when she never, ever let anyone touch her.

'Why are you giving her to me?' I asked, not really wanting to take it.

'Keep it. We're leaving. I can't take her along,' she said.

'Leaving? Where to?'

'Maybe India, maybe Nepal. But away from here. Baba said the road is long and we need to carry only food and things for the journey. Since we have to walk a long distance, Gudia won't be able to come along,' she said.

'You love Gudia so much. You made her. I'm sure you can carry her with you,' I said.

'I'll have to carry rice and some clothes. Ma has to carry my baby brother. Baba will carry my toddler sister and all the other stuff on his back. Baba says there's no space in the bags for Gudia,' she said. Tears filled her eyes.

'Why do you need to leave? We can stay here along the tracks like we always have,' I said.

From a distance, Mariamma must have seen Bidya handing me the doll and came rushing over. 'Bidya, you never let me touch her. Now you're letting Laxmi hold her?'

'Shh, Mariamma, not now,' I whispered into her ear. 'Bidya is leaving.'

Bidya pulled out two coconut shells wrapped in a rag and a few tiny clay utensils we had made to play with and handed them to Mariamma. The coconut shells were the prized utensils of our kitchen set. We would not only pretend to cook in them with leaves and water, but we would build structures with them too. First, we'd have to mix mud and water till it was the right consistency—not too watery, not too dry. We would fill the coconut shell with the mixture and overturn it on the ground, and gently pull up the coconut shell, to get a mound of the shape of the shell. We made several such mounds and created buildings like the golden pagodas in Burma. Honestly, I would have preferred the coconut shells to the scary doll.

But I didn't want to ask Mariamma to swap and hurt Bidya's feelings. She was already so heartbroken.

'Bidya! O Bidya!' Her father had come looking for her. Perhaps my baba had been listening to our conversation because he quickly joined us when he saw Bidya's father. 'Are you leaving? Why? Where? When?' Baba asked.

Bidya's father simply said, 'We have to leave. All of you too should think of leaving.' He looked quite glum.

'What are you saying?' Baba said. By now, Mariamma's father had walked up to us all.

'There are whispers that the British are losing Burma to the Japanese. The British Army will withdraw soon. We all need to hurry.'

'But how can we go? The British have stopped the sale of ship tickets to Indians. They don't want us to leave. We're trapped,' Baba said.

'It's only the poor Indians who are trapped,' said Mariamma's father. 'They'd stopped selling tickets for the lower decks to prevent working-class Indians from leaving Burma. Tickets for the upper decks are available, but we can't afford them. Only rich businessmen and moneylenders can buy those tickets and go back. Many from Rangoon have already left. But if the British are also leaving now, they may not mind the working-class Indians leaving. Maybe tickets for the lower berths will start.'

'But with so many people vying for tickets, lower-berth prices will shoot up. There's no way we can be sure of getting them,' Baba said,

'But we can walk. We can walk all the way to our homes. That's what we intend to do,' Bidya's father declared.

'Walk? It's too far. There are jungles and high mountains along the way. There's no straight path,' Baba said.

'Yes, but we're mountain people. We grew up in the mountains. I think we can manage,' Bidya's father said.

'What route are you taking?' Mariamma's father asked.

'We're taking the Hukawng Valley route, going through Pangsau Pass towards Ledo in the north and entering the plains of Assam,' he replied.

'You mean you're taking the Death Valley route?'

'What do you mean?' Baba asked.

'Wait here a minute,' Mariamma's father said before rushing to his hut. He returned with a young, frail-looking man. His skin hung loose on his bones. It looked as if he could take it off like a piece of loose clothing. 'He's my nephew Murli,' Mariamma's father said. 'He used to work at a moneylender's house in Rangoon. The family left by steamer, abandoning the servants.' Murli looked puzzled as to why he had been dragged into this conversation between the older men.

'Tell them. Tell them what you saw and heard. Tell them about your journey,' Mariamma's father said to him.

Murli fidgeted with the fold of his lungi while speaking. 'My friends and I intended to walk and take Tamu Pass and enter the Imphal valley, but we turned around midway.'

Bidya's father interrupted. 'The Japanese have already begun occupying those parts along that route.'

'Yes. Moreover, the trails are crowded. It's not just bombs and attacks that we need to be careful of, but also diseases. So, we decided to go northwards and take another route. It was the same there too. The trails were lined with corpses. Some had died due to fatigue. They couldn't endure the trek any longer. Some died from starvation. The water bodies along the way are polluted and infected, so cholera is widespread. Bullocks and mules tied to carts have also not been able to endure the journey. People, in desperation, have resorted to eating the meat of these dead animals. The air is filled with a strange smell ... the stench of rotting bodies. Some say thousands of families have perished on this trek to India. The British are calling it the Death Valley,' Murli said.

'You endured all that and still found the strength to walk back to Rangoon and find your way here?' Bidya's father sounded doubtful.

Mariamma's father chimed in. 'When there is no other hope, one obviously turns to relatives, isn't it? I'm only trying to caution you. Don't suspect our intentions.'

'It's okay, Uncle. His doubt is genuine,' said Murli gently.

'Yes, if you'd already gone that far, why return? You could have kept going ahead instead of turning back,' Bidya's father said.

Murli spoke up at this point. 'On our way, we spotted a motor vehicle returning to Burma. It was going to pick up a European family, but the driver was Indian. We requested him to give us a ride back.'

'In that case, we can find motor vehicles to take us to India, isn't it?' Baba asked.

'No, not us,' Murli replied. 'Motor vehicles are reserved only for Europeans, even if they are non-British. But Indians are supposed to walk or use bullock carts. Even the trails are different for them and for us. The roads they take are better. We have to go through the narrow trails through the forest.'

'We're as good as cattle to them,' Mariamma's father said. 'They herded us here, made us work and abandoned us. And now, they're discriminating even during an escape from a war. Their war!'

'We should never have come here. This is not our country. There's no place for us here,' Bidya's father said.

No amount of coaxing was going to stop Bidya's family from leaving. Her father had made up his mind. They left the next morning before we'd even woken up. Their rooster was the one who woke up the colony with its crowing at the crack of dawn. That morning, it didn't. Perhaps they took it along. Perhaps they carried its meat. Bidya's mom's chicken pickle was famous. Perhaps she pickled the rooster for their journey.

As the days passed, more people left. Our colony was reduced to half of what it had once been. Since so many huts were left unoccupied, we pulled out parts of their thatch or the supporting canes and used them to repair our own homes. Food was becoming scarce. Second helpings of rice stopped, and then each family member would get just one ladle of rice. Slowly, we got down to eating just one meal a day. And Ma's dal became paler day by day, until we were one day served just rice with warm water.

Since all of Nakul's friends had left, he constantly hung around Mariamma and me, trying to get us to play with him. It got pretty annoying. While he was free to play all day, we girls were allowed to play only after we had helped our mothers with the chores. 'Finish the sweeping. Only then can you go out to play,' Ma would tell me. Since Nakul was always hovering around us, Mariamma and I could not even speak in private. We would sneak into Bidya's abandoned hut to hide from Nakul.

'Do you think Bidya has reached Assam?' Mariamma asked one day.

'I don't know,' I replied. 'I dreamt of her the other night. She was walking all alone with her doll, stepping on skulls along the path. She kept looking around and unknowingly stepped off a cliff and fell. That scared me awake.'

'What do you think it meant? Amma says dreams always have meanings. Maybe they're warnings,' Mariamma said.

'I don't want to think of them as warnings. That's scary. I hope Bidya is safe. I hope she's not alone.'

'I hope so too,' replied Mariamma. 'I guess I'll never be alone again.' She sighed deeply.

'What do you mean?' I asked.

'Appa has promised me in marriage to our relative Murli.'

'Murli! That cousin who returned from Death Valley?'

'Obviously him,' she said, sounding cross. 'How many other relatives of mine called Murli do you know?'

'How can you get married? You're only my age. Maybe just a year or two older,' I objected.

'Amma says they will marry me off as soon as I "come of age", whatever that means. Then, I'll be sent on the ship with Murli to go and live with his family. Amma says it'll be easy for me to adjust since we're already family,' she said.

'I don't like this idea one bit. Do you realise you'll have to swap the coconut shells for real utensils? Cook in a real kitchen? You won't have the time to play with me,' I said.

'That's scary to think about.' Mariamma chewed on her lower lip, blinking hard. 'Amma says we need to move quickly. It's war time, so they may not be able to find a better match for me later.'

'Why don't you talk to your amma–appa again? Your appa will listen to you.'

'This was his idea. Amma is a bit more worried—she doesn't want me to face the same troubles she faced. She also got married when she was my age.'

'Is there no way you can get out of this?' I asked.

'Maybe if I run away, but where will I run to? If I leave home on my own, I'll either be killed or kidnapped.'

'Why does your appa want to marry you off?'

'He says he's doing this because he loves me. He can afford only two lower deck tickets: one for me and one for Murli. But we will have to take along Chinnu.' Chinnu was Mariamma's baby brother. 'He cannot let me go with Murli if we aren't married,' she continued. 'So I will travel as his wife and we will pretend Chinnu is our baby. Amma–Appa will stay here until they save enough to buy tickets to India for themselves.'

As the bombings went on, more British officers left. Since there were barely any of them left, we Indians were no longer needed for work, so the ticket sales were opened once again. It was time for Mariamma to leave.

She was wearing her mom's red saree. It seemed to weigh more than she did herself. She hugged me, Chinnu cradled in one arm, but didn't say a word. Maybe the words were stuck in her throat. And anyway, Murli was in a hurry. 'Let's go. How long are you taking? Come on!' I didn't like his tone. He seemed so different from when I first saw him. I felt sorry for Mariamma, but Ma said, 'This is how it is for girls. A woman has to respect and obey her husband, no matter what.'

'But that's unfair, Ma!' I said.

'That's how it is. That's how it's been since the beginning of time.'

'How do you know that? You weren't around at the beginning of time.'

'Don't answer back. Get to work. You also have to learn to cook well. Get in the kitchen now,' she ordered. Nakul smirked and went off to play.

Chapter 3

GIANT BIRDS AND EGGS OF FIRE

One evening, news arrived that the Japanese had taken over Burma and the British Army had gone back to India. We were all relieved. 'At last, there will be no more bombings from the sky,' Ma said.

We didn't care who ruled Burma. It could have been the British, the Japanese or the Burmese. All we wanted was peace. The days started getting a little easier. We went back to sitting around the bonfire and cooking on the choolah outdoors. But finding work wasn't easy for Indians. Many Burmese looked at us as outsiders stealing their jobs. For others, it wasn't just about work. They had had bad experiences with Indian moneylenders, and decided to dislike all of us.

Some people from Ma–Baba's village in India, who also worked with them and stayed with us in the same colony, decided to return home on foot. Ma felt that we too should leave and start walking, if steamer services had stopped with the increased intensity of war, but Baba didn't agree.

'The journey through the jungles is treacherous. And it's not even just wild creatures we'd have to protect ourselves from but diseases too. Haven't you heard the stories? What's going on is another World War! What if the British want to reclaim Burma and we get caught in the crossfire while travelling back to India? That too with two young children,' Baba said to Ma.

Ma, like always, would agree and find something magical to say: 'Our elders say that the road to heaven is a difficult one, riddled with obstacles. Our homeland is no less than paradise. We will return when the kids are strong enough to endure the journey.' I'm not sure if she said this to reassure us or to hide her helplessness. For Nakul and me, Burma was the only home we had known. As long as we could eat, play and sleep, and had Ma–Baba's company, we were happy.

Ma began sharing more stories of her village, the nearby towns, the people and mysteries of the surrounding forests. My favourite was the one about the morning Ma and her sister had gone to the fields to cut some grass for the cattle. They spotted two demon heads dancing above a fence. No bodies. Just heads with long fangs and bulging eyes. Ma said, 'The first thought in my mind was to use my sickle and cut the head of the rakshas if it attacked us. Then I realised, what would I behead? It was already beheaded. There was no torso, no legs. Just two laughing heads bobbing in the air.'

Nakul's eyes were wide. 'What did you do, Ma?' he asked.

'We figured since the heads had not attacked us, we should quietly leave. Why trouble something that hasn't troubled us?'

'And then, Ma? Then?'

'Wait. Do you remember what I told you about not disturbing anything if it's not bothering you?' she reminded us.

'Yes, Ma,' I replied. 'Like not to bother a snake if we spot it sleeping, or in its burrow, or if it's just passing by.' Snakes were very frequently seen around our house. Sometimes, they'd be in the piles of firewood. Sometimes, we would find their shed skin around the house.

'Right. Don't poke it with a stick, or throw stones, or try to chase it. If it senses danger, it will attack you to protect itself. If not, it won't trouble you.' Ma always found ways to remind us of these things through her stories. 'Snakes don't see humans as food like they do rats and frogs. They won't attack you without reason. So it's important that you do nothing that may make them feel threatened.'

'Ma, get back to the bobbing heads! What happened next?' Nakul said.

'I decided to back away quietly and return home. But my sister was naughty like you, Nakul. And curious too. She wondered what would happen if she threw a stone at them. Would the heads fall down?'

'Did she do it?' I asked.

'She pulled out her catapult, aimed at one of the heads and took a shot. The head opened its mouth and gobbled the stone.'

'But if the heads didn't have bodies, where did the stone go?' I asked.

'It dropped out from the bottom of the head. From the ground, where the stone had hit the earth, a body started forming—a torso, two large arms, heavy, bulky legs. The body attached itself to the head. The rakshas was whole again.'

Nakul and I stared at Ma, both scared and excited. 'Did you both run?' I asked.

'We did, but it walked towards us, taking giant strides. We couldn't get far. We felt his footsteps shaking the earth as he got closer. We felt his breath on the back of our heads like a gush of wind. I shouted to my sister, "We will not be able to outrun it. Let's face it instead of running away," and we both turned.'

'Then? What happened next?' asked Nakul.

'The demons were angry. The air they puffed out of their nostrils was as strong as a hurricane. We were sent flying and hit a banyan tree. We held on to the hanging roots of the banyan and tried to slide down slowly. If we'd lost our grip, we would have fallen from that great height. But the rakshas wrapped one of the roots around us and tied us to a branch.'

'Like a jackfruit or a mango?' Nakul asked. 'I mean, were you tied like a jackfruit that grows on the trunk or like a mango that grows on the branch.'

'Like coconuts in a bunch,' Ma replied. 'We were bundled together, hanging from the top of the tree.'

'But the last time you told us this story, you said you were both sitting on the branch and dangling your legs, the tops of your thighs tied to the tree,' Nakul said.

'Oh, that! I didn't want to scare by saying we were so high up. You've grown taller now, so the top of the tree shouldn't seem too high to you,' she said. I knew Ma liked to change some of the details of her stories, or perhaps she forgot exactly what she had narrated each time. I doubted any of these stories had ever happened in real life, but I loved listening to them anyway, imagining each scene in my mind.

'What happened after that? How did you get down, Ma?' Though he had heard the story many times, he also clearly enjoyed the new twists Ma added.

'We were both scared. My sister began to weep. I told her to keep quiet and not panic. The best thing in such situations is to remain calm, because only then can you think clearly. I mustered up my courage and asked the rakshas why he was angry. He replied, "Because she hit me with a stone."'

'Your sister shouldn't have hit him, Ma,' Nakul said, shaking his head in disapproval.

'But that wasn't the time to feel guilty. We needed to think on our feet. So I immediately told him, "We want to help you."'

'Did he believe you?' Nakul asked.

'At first, he didn't. He snarled and bared his teeth. I trembled.'

'What about the other bobbing head? Was he a rakshas too?'

'Yes, the other rakshas with just the bobbing head was thinking this whole time. He thundered, "Wait! Shoot a stone at me too."'

'Why would he ask you to hit him, Ma?' Nakul said.

'The rakshas with the body asked him the same thing. The head replied, "After they shot you with the stone, a body grew from where the stone landed. They helped you regain your body." The rakshas with the body who had tied us to the tree suddenly realised this. His eyes sparkled. He immediately thanked us and unbound us.'

Nakul opened his mouth in shock, as though this was all brand new to him. 'Did you run?' he asked.

'No, there was no point in running. They would catch us immediately. Attack or flight are not always the right responses. Here, they were ready to talk. So we listened. They asked us to help the other rakshas regain his body.'

'Did you help?' asked Nakul.

'Yes, they did. They had no choice, did they?' I chimed in.

Ma continued, 'We first stepped back to aim properly, and then I shot. The head quickly opened his mouth and gobbled the stone, which fell from its neck to the ground. And then—'

'Two legs and two arms grew out of the ground,' I interrupted.

Ma shook her head. 'No, that didn't happen.'

'Then what happened?' Nakul said impatiently. 'Did they attack you?'

'No. Four legs with claws and two mighty wings sprouted, along with the body of a lion. It rose and attached itself to the head. A lion's body with wings and a human-looking head with sharp fangs. The two demons laughed loudly. "Ha ha ha!" The earth shook beneath them with each guffaw. Then the rakshas with the human body mounted the other rakshas with the lion's body and together they flew away.'

'Simply flew away? Didn't they grant you any boon?' Nakul asked.

'They did. They told me that I would get a loving husband and two sweet children—one strong daughter like the lion rakshas and one courageous son like the human rakshas,' she said, kissing our foreheads and tucking us into bed. Ma's stories helped us sleep, making us forget that we hadn't had any dinner. The stories helped us dream and relish the one meal Ma–Baba could provide us daily.

Unlike Ma's stories, the tales Baba told were usually all about facts. It seemed like he wanted to teach us about different subjects, people and places. He too spoke of the magical land that Bharat is. One day, he pointed to the sky and said, 'This is how tall Lord Jagannath's temple is in Puri.'

'As tall as me, Baba?' asked Nakul, who was only as tall as a shrub.

'Much taller,' replied Baba.

'Then as tall as Lakhmi?' he asked. I was only a little taller than the rose shrub at gora saheb's house. 'Or as tall as you, Baba?' Nakul continued.

Baba smiled 'Taller than me. Taller than the banyan. Taller than the peepal.'

'Taller than the Indian seth's house in Rangoon?' asked Nakul.

'Yes, taller even than the clock tower in the market.' If Baba was getting as annoyed with Nakul's guesses as I was, he didn't show it. He pointed to the sky again and said, 'Look up. The temple is even taller than—' but a loud, whistling sound cut him off. It was coming from the sky.

'Birds! Giant birds!' I screamed.

'The birds are pooping,' yelled Nakul. 'They're dropping bird poop. Perhaps they ate too much chilli.'

'No, it looks like a huge egg,' I said. It took us some time to gather our senses. Baba hadn't said anything all this time. He was just looking around wildly. The first egg fell on the railway line and burst into a ball of fire.

'Run! Hide! Get away from the railway line. Get away from the houses. Run into the forest,' Baba screamed over his shoulder, running towards our house to wake Ma up. Nakul and I took off.

When I looked back, I saw our hut in flames. 'Nakul, look!' I yelled. We stopped and turned around, but a burning tree crashed down and blocked the path back to our house. I ran towards a ditch that the gora sahebs had made us dig to take shelter in case of an air bombing, and jumped into it. Before this, I didn't know what an air bombing looked like. I hadn't imagined it to be so horrendous.

The bombings continued until the railway lines were reduced to twisted bars of iron, and our huts along the rail line were turned into embers. The whistling sound of the falling bombs kept echoing in my ears. It was as if the shrill sound entered our ears, twisted our nerves and stopped our brains from working. I didn't hear any screams, nor did I scream myself. I just peered over the edge of the ditch and watched the flames.

It took me a while to return to my senses and look for Nakul. He had jumped into the ditch with me, hadn't he? Didn't he run with me? Or did he run some other way? It was all blurry. 'Nakul! Nakul! Nakku!' I called out. The ringing in my ears slowly faded, and I started hearing other people's screams. 'What if Ma–Baba need help?' I thought and went around the burning tree to my home. Nothing remained of the hut except for a pile of ashes. There was no sight of Ma–Baba. Had they escaped? I hoped they had. As I looked around for them, a familiar glint caught my eye—Ma's bangle, lodged in a charred piece of wood.

I went closer. Suddenly, my view changed. Everything was burnt beyond recognition. I looked upwards. The sky was empty. All the trees had fallen. One lonely tree stump stood burning like a torch. I felt sick with fear. I stumbled backwards, my eyes still fixed on the ashes of our hut. My foot grazed against something. The half-burnt doll Bidya had gifted me. I ran. I ran until I couldn't breathe. I sat down in the dirt, panting, my heart pounding against my chest, my vision blurry with tears. The world was spinning around me.

Nakul had passed out. I found him lying motionless under a tree. A Burmese woman I had often seen collecting firewood but whom I'd never spoken to was squatting next to him, sprinkling water on his face. 'Is he dead?' I asked her quietly in Burmese.

'No, he's in shock,' she replied. 'Do you know him?'

'He's my younger brother,' I said.

'Ah, good.' She stood up slowly. 'Take good care of him.' She began limping away.

'What do I do?' I asked her helplessly.

'Sprinkle some water on his face. Here, keep this pot. Be with him. He will live.'

I tried to follow her instructions, but my fingers weren't cooperating and didn't move the way they should have. They felt frozen, as if all my fear had settled in them. My chest felt tight. I lay down beside Nakul in the dirt. Would he wake up? If he did, what would we do next? Where would we go? Tears rolled down my cheeks from my tightly shut eyes. I had seen enough.

Chapter 4

THE TRAIN ON THE FLOOR

'Lakhmi? Lakhmi! Are you dead? Are you alive? Please wake up. Please don't be dead.' Someone was slapping my face. Nakul was crouching over me. I rubbed my eyes and let out a sigh of relief. He was alive.

'I'm glad you're not dead, Lakhmi,' he said. I smiled. I wanted to tell him how worried I had been, how happy I was that he was okay. Instead, I hugged him, not wanting to let go.

Dusk was setting in. The embers from the huts still burnt. Nakul and I walked back to where our home used to be. Though he didn't say anything out loud, I knew Nakul was thinking about Ma–Baba, just like I was. We needed to find them. Ma would be worried and waiting for us. Baba would probably be repairing our hut.

When we reached closer, we spotted some soldiers. Some were Burmese, some Japanese. 'No survivors. All ash,' I heard someone saying in Burmese. Sometimes, even when you know something deep down, a part of you doesn't believe it until someone else confirms it. Though I had feared Ma–Baba had died, the man's words confirmed it, like the gong of a bell.

I didn't want Nakul to hear anything, so I covered his ears with my palms. But he looked up at me, tears rolling down his face, and said, 'I heard.' I knew I couldn't break down in front of Nakul but my eyes welled up. I turned away and blinked hard, looking up at the sky.

'Get away from here. Hide. Don't let the Japanese soldiers see you,' whispered the Burmese woman from behind. We were startled. I hadn't seen her after she had given me the water and left. Had she been around all this while? Was she hiding? Our minds were too fuzzy to process what was happening around.

'The Japanese soldiers take away girls and make them their slaves. Stay away from them,' she said and signalled for us to follow her. She hid behind a tree and continued to watch the soldiers.

'Why did the Japanese bomb us? We didn't do anything,' Nakul said.

'It wasn't them. The British bombed this rail line,' she muttered.

'But why? We worked for them. Why would they bomb our homes?' he asked.

'I don't think the target was your homes or any home. It must have been the train tracks. They may have wanted to destroy all the communication and rail lines. The British don't want the Japanese to use what they built. Now they have American support too. I overheard the soldiers say that American planes are bombing Burma.'

I wondered where she was taking us. What about our neighbours from the colony? Had anyone else survived? Were we the only ones? 'Where are the others?' I asked her.

'Who others?'

'Other people. Somebody apart from just us must have survived this.'

'I don't know about them. I'm not out here rescuing everyone. I just found you two with your arms and legs intact. Bombs do more than just hit the ground—they bring fire, flying pieces and total mess. All your thatched huts didn't stand a chance. You're lucky you weren't inside. People scattered and ran helter-skelter. If anyone else survived, they must have gone in some other direction.'

I was still worried. What if this was some kind of trick? What if she was leading us to a trap? 'How do you know so much about bombings?' I asked.

She sighed. 'Because we survived it when the Japanese bombed Burma. We moved to this forest to escape bombings and the war. But they seemed to have followed us here too.'

'What kind of work do you do?' I asked.

She laughed at that. 'Is there any work that you Indians have left for us? You entered Burma in a swarm, ready to work for less money, and took away all our jobs. And the Indian moneylenders have squished every ounce of blood from us Burmese borrowers. They've taken our land and left us penniless.' Her expression grew angry. 'It's not just the British that we want out. It's the Indians too.'

I tried not to show it, but I was terrified. Her words were so cutting. Ma used to say, 'Beware of the ones whose words are dipped in honey. They are the ones waiting to sting.' At least this woman wasn't trying to sweet-talk us. Her bitter words meant she didn't care if we followed her or not. She clearly wasn't trying to trick us.

'Why did you help us then?' I asked.

'I did nothing. It's you two who are following me,' she snapped.

'But you asked us to,' Nakul piped up.

She didn't answer but kept walking, stepping over rocks and bending to avoid the forest's branches.

'At least the British and most of us Indians are out of Burma. You must be glad,' I said.

'Now the Japanese have occupied Burma. They have the Burma Independence Army backing them, but it's the Japanese who are ruling us. They haven't been kind to us locals. The truth is that this is not freedom. Burma will be free only when we have self-rule, without any outside influence. We need a complete Burmese government. No British. No Japanese. No foreigners.'

When we came to a clearing, we saw some dilapidated huts. They were our homes. Our old homes. We lived there back when the railway construction was happening in that part. We moved to the other end of the forest when the tracks had to be laid ahead. We'd keep shifting, moving along the new tracks.

'That one over there is mine.' The woman pointed to a hut to the far right. 'You can pick any of the others. From now on, you're on your own.' She didn't wait for a response before walking towards her house.

Nakul and I looked at each other, confused.

'Do you remember which one was our house?' I asked.

'They all look the same, Lakhmi,' he replied. 'I was so small then. I don't remember clearly.'

Trying to remember our old home was so difficult. My mind was getting weighed down with memories of Ma–Baba here. It felt like being lost in the fog and trying to catch a white feather floating just out of reach. Have you ever tried that? Catching a white feather in the middle of a thick fog? I once did. I stretched my arm out and thought I'd caught it. But when I unclenched my fist, there was nothing there. But I knew the feather was there, so I tried again and again until I finally managed to grab it. It's the same with a memory. You know it's somewhere in your mind, so you keep trying to recall it, until you finally manage to catch hold of the memory.

I had finally remembered something that would help me recognise our house.

One rainy day, when we couldn't play out side, Nakul and I were bored at home. Nakul was getting really restless. So Ma cleaned the floor, which she had levelled and smeared with cow dung. With a piece of chalk, she drew a train with box-like bogies. We had to throw a stone into the first box and hop onto it, standing only on one leg. Using the leg we were standing on, we then had to kick the stone to the second box and do it all over again. This went on until the stone was out of the train. If we ever put a leg down, we'd be out. Nakul and I played turn by turn. The chalk marks would keep getting erased by our feet, and Ma would redraw the train bogies each time. One day, Baba got some chuna from work. He mixed the limestone with water and used it to paint the train, making our game permanent.

'Nakul, do you remember the train? The train Ma drew and that Baba painted?' I asked. 'The one we used for our hopping game?'

'Yes! I remember hopping on one leg and kicking a flat stone,' he said.

'The design must be on the floor of one of these houses. Let's find our old house and stay there,' I said.

We dashed in and out of the worn-down huts, peeking under fallen roofs and sweeping away dry leaves, our eyes straining in the faint light of the setting sun. After we had checked out five or six huts, it had become dark. The sun had set. We decided to try one last hut and there it was—the white outline of a train sparkling in the moonlight. No leaves and twigs covering the floor, unlike in the other huts. It felt like Ma–Baba were there with us, guiding us. Welcoming us home. The thatched roof had a big hole in it, so when Nakul and I lay down, we could see the stars through it.

'Ma–Baba are watching over us. See those two stars? That's them,' I told Nakul. He clutched my arm and nodded. Neither one of us spoke for the rest of the night. We slept on the train, feeling Ma–Baba's warmth around us.

Chapter 5

THE MADAM WHO HID HER NAME

As the sun rose, I woke up to the crow of Bidya's rooster—or so I thought. It was just a dream. My mind had replaced the cawing ravens outside with the rooster. I wondered if Bidya's family had survived the journey. And was Mariamma still on the ship with Chinnu? Was Murli treating her well? Both my friends had gone. And Ma–Baba had gone farther than them all.

The house looked different in the light of the sun. It had felt warm at night, but now it seemed cold and empty. The roof was ready to fall, the hole looking much bigger than it had when we first saw it. A group of crows looked through it, watching us. Nakul was still asleep. I wanted to tell him not to worry, that Ma–Baba were with us, that maybe they had sent the crows themselves. But I held my tongue. If Nakul decided to start asking hundreds of questions, it would be exhausting. A curious Nakul is far more annoying than a sulking Nakul. Anyway, first I would have to deal with a hungry Nakul when he woke up. I patted him and said, 'Sleep, Nakul. Sleep a little more.' But suddenly, one of the crows swooped down through the roof, flapping its wings right in Nakul's face, and grabbed a rat from the corner before flying away.

Nakul woke up startled. 'What was that?'

I pointed to the crows above us. 'One flew down to take a rat,' I said.

'But why are they watching us? I was fast asleep. Did they think I would eat the rat? Chhee ... Do the crows think we're after their food now? How horrible!' he sobbed.

'Oh no, not at all. Don't be silly,' I said, trying to calm him.

'Ma would never have called me silly. She would have explained,' he said, sobbing even louder.

I realised then that I could no longer be just the elder sister, always snubbing and arguing with my younger brother. I had to be like Ma: soothing, caring and always ready with a kind reply. I had to *be* Ma.

I wondered what Ma would do. She would probably have told us a story about a crow in her village and a young boy who tamed it and made it his pet.

Nakul suddenly jumped up in excitement. 'Lakhmi, do you remember Ma told us about a white crow? It was a royal crow that stayed in the palace grounds. One day, it stole the queen's pearl necklace and ate the pearls. But it didn't know that the necklace was magical. The pearls turned the crow black. The special crow lost its bright white colour and became a common black crow. Nobody recognised it anymore and it was shooed away. Remember that story, Lakhmi?'

I smiled. Nakul had grown up overnight. He was trying his best to be helpful. He was trying to look out for me just as much as I was for him.

'Let's go find some food, Nakul,' I said.

We stepped out of our hut and found ourselves amidst tall trees all around. There was no clear path. When we lived here with Ma–Baba, I remembered the surroundings were clearer. Now, the creepers and bushes seem to have taken over the land. The roots of the tall trees seem to have crawled ahead like fingers and grasped more earth. Though these surroundings were once familiar, we now felt lost. We looked around and spotted the Burmese woman, whose name we didn't know. She too had stepped out of the hut she had spent the night in and was heading towards the thicket. She noticed us and again signalled us to follow her.

'What's your name?' I asked.

'Why do you want to know? You don't need to know my name,' she said.

'What do we call you then?

'Nothing.'

'Okay, Nothing. Thank you for helping us, Nothing,' Nakul said, sniggering.

'No, I meant …' The woman sighed. 'All right, you know what? You can call me Madam.'

'Why would we call you Madam? We don't work for you. You're not our boss,' I said.

'Yes, but I'm much older than you two, so you should pay me some respect. You're not related to me, so I don't want you to call me anything like aadaw, which would mean aunt in Burmese, or any name in your language that would make other people think we're family. And anyway, I always wanted someone to call me Madam, the way the British ladies were addressed. Feels good,' she said, her hands on her hips.

I thought about it for a few seconds before saying, 'All right, Madam.'

Pleased, Madam direct us into the forest. While the trees towered over us, the ground was covered with grass and weed that grew up to our knees. We placed each step cautiously, hoping not to step on a snake or a scorpion. Madam then began pointing out the plants we could eat and the ones that were poisonous, would make us itch, left rashes, the ones that popped and made a funny sound, that could get stuck in your hair, the ones that were used as medicine.

She pointed out more and more. 'This one is sweet. This one is bitter. This grows in the rainy season, but beware of snakes if you go to pluck it. This one can heal dysentery, and this one can upset your stomach.'

She pointed to some mushrooms. 'These are edible'—she pointed to a different group—'but these are poisonous. In fact, it's best to avoid mushrooms completely. It's not easy to tell which ones are okay to eat, so you may end up eating a poisonous one. Stay away from them. You can survive without them.'

Next up was some grass that had to be burnt in the evening to drive away mosquitoes. 'They hate the smoke from this grass, so they pinch their noses close and fly away,' she said.

'Do they have hands?' Nakul asked.

'Haven't you seen a mosquito up-close?' she asked.

'I have, but they're so tiny. I've never figured out if they have hands,' he replied.

'Next time, watch a mosquito very carefully. They use their two front legs like hands. They rub them like we do'—she rubbed her palms together—'and they hold things too.'

'But they don't have fingers,' Nakul said. 'How can they hold their noses closed?'

'You can't see their fingers because they're even tinier than their hands. But trust me, they have them,' she replied.

I knew Madam was teasing Nakul, but he seemed to be enjoying it. I didn't mind one bit—I was getting a break from having to reply to Nakul's questions.

Madam led us through a narrow pathway, which seemed to have formed by constant walking in the direction. Grass was bent along the way, the shrubs broken and, in some patches, grass had stopped growing. It seemed like it was a regular path Madam took. After a short distance, the soil underneath felt wet, and we heard the gurgling sound of water. We had reached a small, bubbling spring, which flowed down the rocks. The path of the clear gleaming water was as wide as my arm. 'Look, this water springs out directly from the earth's heart,' Madam said, pointing to where the spring danced up from the rocks. 'See how it bubbles out, eager to explore the world?' She drank from it. 'You try it too,' she insisted. It felt heavenly. I drank eagerly and then stepped into the stream. The touch of fresh water washed away all the dust and dirt from the previous day. Nakul jumped in and out of the stream like a tadpole.

'Always drink fresh running water. This spring is perfect to drink from. Don't ever drink from a water source that is stagnant. It could be polluted and give you diseases like cholera, or it could even have been poisoned by enemies,' Madam warned us.

We filled water in the earthen pots Madam had brought with her and stuffed leaves in a basket that she carried on her back.

On returning to the huts, we lit a small fire using dry twigs and boiled the leaves in one of the pots. We drank the soup and ate the cooked leaves. But it didn't keep us full for long, and late at night, we felt hungry again. Nakul and I chewed on some twigs until we fell asleep in our hut, lying down on the drawing of the train.

The days passed with us gathering leaves, herbs and water, and playing in the spring. On some days, Madam went into town to sell the medicinal herbs, and with the money she got, she'd buy rice. She'd give us a little rice as payment for helping her gather herbs. But on days nobody bought herbs from her, she would return angry and wouldn't talk to us. Those nights we went hungry because we were scared of offending her by cooking. We learnt this the hard way. When she came back to the huts one evening with no rice, Nakul and I lit the fire and boiled some leaves in water. She grew furious and kicked the pot. 'Why are you even here? Go! Find your own way. Why should I have you foreigners here burdening me?' she yelled.

'But we help you collect herbs and cook,' Nakul mumbled.

'What "cook"? You just boil some leaves in water. That's all,' she shot back.

I decided to stay quiet, but Nakul replied, 'Not just leaves. Sometimes, you ask us to add roots and mushrooms. Even though you collect the mushrooms, we wash them in the spring, the way you showed us.'

'You're doing that more for yourself. Aren't you eating the same food?' she said.

'We carry the water also. You drink from it too.'

'Don't be so ungrateful, boy!' she shouted. 'If not for me, you two would have been dead already. I've been protecting you from the Japanese and keeping you safe from British bombings. The world is at war. I'm the one who has provided you safety.'

Of course, we were thankful to her for saving us and teaching us how to survive, but we didn't like it when she rubbed it in our faces. It felt like she wanted us to be her slaves. And we never knew which version of Madam we would get each day. On some days she was kind, but on other days she was just awful. Nakul and I had to be extremely careful around her. Anything we said or did that she didn't like would throw her into a fit. We wished she would explain the dos and don'ts of interacting with her the way she had done the forest. That would have made life around her easier.

Whenever she went into town, we felt like we could stop holding our breath. Without her around, we cooked leaves and ate fruits, but we'd pretend to be hungry when we saw her at the end of the day. But one day, when she returned empty-handed, Nakul, being himself, blurted out, 'We don't need rice, anyway. We cooked some leafy soup.'

Madam stared at us, her eyes blazing in anger, her fists clenched. 'You, ungrateful wretches! I should have let you both rot,' she yelled and then stormed off. She didn't talk to us for all of the next day. Even though we could have cooked something for ourselves, Nakul and I went hungry. Maybe it was to make up for having eaten in her absence.

The next day, she must have felt sorry for us, because she took us to a rice mill, where rice grains were separated from the chaff. We sat huddled where the chaff was dumped and went through it, looking for rice grains that had mistakenly got mixed with the chaff. We collected these grains and brought them home to make rice. We even brought some chaff to eat when we had nothing else. Madam was kind at heart, but her mood swings turned her into a completely different person. One thing never changed, though. She would keep singing her own praises. 'I must have a golden heart to have taken you two foreign orphans in.'

'What do you mean? You just pointed to these huts and told us to pick,' Nakul once said.

'I should have left you to the leopards and tigers. They would have loved to crunch on your bones,' she said, her eyes narrowing.

I squeezed Nakul's hand as a sign. Then I began complimenting her. 'If not for you, we would have been inside a python's belly! You're our saviour!' It was the only thing I could think to do to calm her down.

Chapter 6

THE FROG KINGDOM

One morning, Nakul couldn't pull himself out of bed. I noticed how thin and weak he had become. I could see the shape of his bones under his skin. 'I'm too tired to get up, Lakhmi,' he mumbled.

I rushed to Madam's hut. 'Please help Nakul. He says he's too tired to get out of bed,' I pleaded.

'I was worried this would happen. I saw him stumbling yesterday. He's not tired—he's weak. Fatigued. He needs to get some strength. You cannot live on leaves alone,' she said.

'What can I give him? Is there a plant that can help?' I begged.

She thought for a few seconds. 'There's something we use for such cases. But we'd have to go to the villages, to the paddy fields, for it. I was trying to avoid that,' she said.

'Please, I'm ready to do anything. Just tell me what we need to do,' I said.

'Frogs. They're good for health and are known to provide strength. We give them to pregnant women too. If he eats one, he'll get his strength back.'

That wasn't what I had expected to hear. 'Frogs? Really?'

'It's the easiest way to get some meat. That's what he needs now, not twigs and leaves,' she said.

Going to catch a frog would mean leaving Nakul on his own. What if someone kidnapped him while I was gone? What if a wild animal attacked him? What if the crows decided they'd had enough of rats and chose him for their next meal? But I had no choice. He needed help fast.

Madam led me along a path that was similar to the path to the stream, narrow with grass and weeds that had been stamped upon. Instead of leading deeper into the forest, the path took us towards grasslands and stopped at the edge of a paddy field. Madam grabbed my hand and pulled me behind a bush. 'Walk slowly into the water, hide behind the paddy and when you see a frog—snatch it up quickly. Put it into this'—she handed me an earthen pot—'and cover it with the lid immediately,' she said.

'Will you not come with me?' I asked.

'I'm taller than you so I won't be able to hide from people as easily as you,' she said.

'Why do you need to hide? They're just frogs. Why would anyone care if you catch them? Aren't they just pests?' I asked.

'We're in the middle of a war. People are without work, without money and without food. Anything to eat is precious,' she said.

'But the farmer has such a large field. He grows grains and may not need to eat frogs,' I said.

'A rich farmer,' she remarked. 'The rich always want to get richer. They have the means and the opportunity for that. The poor just want enough to survive, but they have no means for even that. In this farmer's case, he has paddy. He also has frogs in his field, which eat the insects and pests and keep the paddy healthy. When the population of frogs increases and becomes bothersome, the farmer may hunt and eat them or he may sell these frogs to people like us. He looks at the frogs as resources that can be profited from when needed,' she explained.

All I understood was that she wasn't going to join me in the frog hunt. I sat on the edge of the field, folded my saree above my knees and tied a knot, and slowly slid into the muddy water, which came up to my knees.

'Squat down. Put your hands in the mud. Bend your head closer to the water surface, peer through the water and try to spot a frog. Fumble around and try to feel for a frog,' she instructed. I didn't like being ordered around like this, but I couldn't refuse. I had to do it for Nakul.

'What do frogs feel like?' I asked.

'Cold and slimy. Their skin feels slightly coarse,' she said.

'It's so difficult to catch them without being able to see them,' I said.

'The water's all muddy now since you slid inside with force. When you step forward, go slowly. Don't disturb the earth under you so much. Better still, try to look ahead and spot a frog before moving at all. That way, you can guess its location even if the water gets muddy.'

I moved my hands around wildly but only felt mud. Finally, my fingers touched something. At first, I flinched but then quickly pulled it out. 'Aha!' I said before looking at it. It was a stone.

Madam chuckled. 'Better luck next time.'

I waded ahead, moving the paddy out of my way with my hands, until I spotted a frog. It was sitting on a tiny rock, basking in the sun. I leapt forward, but the frog was too quick for me. I stumbled and fell, my head bouncing off the rock. My forehead started throbbing, but the pain wasn't going to stop me. I had to get that frog. I looked around, one hand on my head, trying to rub the pain away, and the other hand stretched out to catch the frog. There it was, balancing on a paddy stalk. I imagined it chuckling at me like Madam had. I crouched among the itchy paddy stalks, waiting, and then—bam! I quickly grasped it with both hands. 'Madam, I caught it! I caught the frog!' I shrieked.

'Good. Catch more.'

'Isn't one enough?' I asked, hunching down and walking back to the edge of the field.

'No. Catch more.' She came and leaned closer with the pot. I quickly put the frog in it and Madam closed it with a lid.

I went in again, confident now. This time, it took me much less time. I grabbed the second frog before it could leap away and put it into the pot. 'You're getting better,' Madam cheered on from the side. The next time I put my hands back in the water, I felt something slimy and cold. Another frog! I grabbed it and pulled it out. But it wasn't a frog—it was a snake.

'Eee! Ma … Ma!' I screamed and flung it as far as I could. It landed right on Madam's shoulder. She shrieked and jerked until it hit the ground and slithered away.

I ran out. 'I'm not getting into the paddy field again!' I shouted. 'What if the snake had bitten me? Who would look after Nakul then?'

'Relax. It was nothing. Just a rat snake. It's not poisonous' she said.

'What if it had been venomous? What if I died from a snake bite?' I knew I was shouting but I couldn't stop myself—I was too scared. 'Ma used to say even a bite from a non-venomous snake hurts for many days.'

'I told you, it wasn't harmful. It was probably there looking for a frog, just like you were,' Madam said.

'Oh, so now I'm competing with a snake for food?' I asked.

'Well, you are. We all are. Think about it. We compete with boars and bulls for leaves and herbs, with birds and monkeys for fruits, with insects for grains and with snakes for frogs and fish. We also fight our own species too,' she said.

Madam was right. At least animals fight only over food and land. What do humans fight over? This war was so ridiculous. Why did the Japanese have to be in Burma? Why were the Americans involved? And the British—I wished they had never left their kingdom. How nice it would have been if all of them had just stayed in their houses with their families. Instead, everybody was fighting each other like babbler birds in a flock. When these birds argue, you can't tell who is fighting whom. There's just a lot of noise and flapping. We didn't care what the British or Japanese were fighting about. Their war has made me fight snakes for food.

I wanted to give up on the frog hunt, but thinking of Nakul kept me going. An hour later, I had four more.

'We have enough now,' Madam said and turned around to walk back to the huts. I followed her, the pot resting on my hips. She showed me how to clean the frogs, skin them and cut their legs. To me, they looked like human legs with tiny fingers. 'No, they look like chicken legs,' Madam said while we cooked a soup with the frog meat. She divided it into two portions, one for her and the other for us.

I fed Nakul most of the broth and all the flesh. 'Mm, tastes good. Something different,' he mumbled. It was perhaps the change in taste, but he seemed to like it.

'What meat is it?' he asked.

I hesitated a bit and mumbled, 'Frog meat,' expecting him to spit it out. Instead he continued to chew quietly.

That night, I told him a story, the way Ma would tell us stories when we were ill.

'You know what happened today, Nakul?'

'Tell me, tell me.' He seemed to have already got some strength back.

'Madam took me to a paddy field owned by an evil landlord who held a huge gun in his hands. His moustache was long and twirled up at the edges. He had a long, wispy beard that made him look like a goat.'

Nakul laughed. 'Bakra daadhi! Bakra daadhi!' Like a goat's beard! Whenever Nakul found something funny, he would say the same thing over and over again and laugh louder each time. His laugh made me laugh, even when the joke wasn't funny.

I continued the story. 'When he snarled, spit fell from his mouth and the edges of his moustache fluttered. He was scary. Madam was so afraid of getting caught by him that she sent me into the paddy field and hid behind the bushes.'

'That's Madam. She always makes us do things for her. She makes us climb trees and crawl through thorny shrubs for plants. She makes us carry pots of water while she only carries the light herbs. Typical!' he said.

'But she helps us too, doesn't she?' I reminded him.

'That she does. Anyway, tell me what happened today,' he said, excited.

'I dived into the water in the paddy field.'

'And you fell flat! Who dives into a paddy field? There's hardly any water in there,' he said.

'That's what I thought too. Then I kept going down, farther and farther. I went all the way to the netherworld. It was so beautiful—there were frogs of every colour all around me. I wondered what would happen if they all croaked together. As if they'd read my thoughts, they all burst into song at the same time.'

Nakul's eyes widened. 'You mean they croaked at the same time, right?'

'No, they were singing. Well, maybe not exactly singing, but it was like they were humming a lovely tune.'

'Can you hum it?'

'I'll try to remember. It was something like "Hmmm ... hmmm ... hmmmmm."'

He laughed. 'You sound like a buzzing mosquito.'

'Trust me, they were humming beautifully. It's just that my voice isn't the same as theirs.'

'That's true. Even frogs have better voices than you,' he teased.

'You know what? I'm not going to tell you what happened next,' I announced.

'Okay, okay. I won't interrupt you again. Anyway, I have a full stomach after so long, so I'm feeling sleepy,' he said.

'This song of the frogs was magical,' I continued. 'Hypnotic. They stood in two rows, one to my left and one to my right. When I looked straight ahead, I spotted a shiny golden frog in between the two rows, way off in the distance. I walked through the water effortlessly. On reaching closer, I noticed he was wearing a crown and holding a sceptre. Just like in that portrait of the king of England that hung in gora saheb's house. This was a frog king! I immediately bowed to him out of respect. But he said in a booming voice, "How dare you come to my kingdom to hunt frogs. I will have you hanged."

'I pleaded and told him how terribly ill you were and how you needed frog medicine. I said, "You frogs are stronger than us humans. You can survive both on land and in water, unlike us weak humans who can survive only on land. I need your magical nectar to help heal my brother." He stroked his chin and then said, "Yes, I hear the world above the water is becoming unliveable, with fire falling from the skies. But we have a problem here too. If you help us with our problem, I will provide you with some frogs who have rebelled against me and chosen to live on land instead of here in the netherworld." I accepted. I would do anything to save my brother.

'The king then said, "There is a snake up above who is in cahoots with the rebel frogs and hunts *only* the frogs loyal to me. This has made it impossible for any of us to get out of water, even to get a little sun. I want you to get this snake out of our way." I agreed and swam out of the netherworld. It felt good to get some sunlight on my face. I searched the paddy field until I saw the snake slicing through the water. I pounced on it and held it in my hands and turned it round and round in the air and flung it far from the field. It fell straight onto Madam's shoulder like a shawl. She shrieked in terror and trembled. Her scream shocked the evil farmer, who came rushing from across the field. His gun was aimed at Madam and me. The snake too watched the farmer in fear. The farmer was about to shoot, when I jumped, pulled the snake from Madam's shoulder and threw it like an arrow at the farmer. The scared snake's scream pierced the air. Terrified, the farmer screamed, "Aaah!", opening his mouth wide. The snake went straight into his mouth. When I returned to Madam, I saw that her earthen pot was magically filled with rebel frogs. It was my reward. Am I not brave?'

'You're a hero! I can't believe I missed all this. I wish I had been there today,' Nakul said.

'You're a hero too, Nakul. You always have been,' I said, squeezing his hand. 'I want you to get well soon. Then we can go on some heroic adventures together.'

He smiled. 'You're beginning to sound like Ma.'

'Did you like the story? It's incredible, isn't it?' I asked.

'It is. It's like the story Ma told us about Lord Jagannath dancing on Kalinag's hood and freeing the water beings of the snake's terror. I think you were one step away from dancing on the snake's hood,' he said.

'I didn't dance, but I wish you had been there to see me fight the snake. I swung it round and round so fast, as though it were a wet piece of cloth—'

'Stop! Now you're beginning to sound like Madam.'

We both burst into laughter. 'I shouldn't overdo it, right?' I said.

'You don't do it often. Only sometimes. Most often, your stories are just the right length.' Nakul smiled. 'Just like Ma's.'

Chapter 7

SNAILS AND PAPER MONEY

Some days later, Madam took me to another paddy field to pick snails. 'Look in the marshy areas. Some bury themselves in the mud. Pick them out,' she instructed me. This time, Madam also got down on her haunches with me and showed me how to look for them. When we had collected a potful of snails, Madam led me in a direction away from where we lived. 'Let me take you into town today,' she said.

'But Nakul is unwell and alone. He must be waiting for us,' I complained.

'We'll go get some rice,' she said.

At the town market, Madam sat by the roadside with the pot to try and sell the snails.

'Do you think anyone will buy them? People can also pick snails from the fields. They may not want to pay for what they can get from the ground,' I said.

'Not everyone has the time or patience to sit in the mud to do that. There are some who may be willing to pay for them,' she said.

People passed by, some curious, some sneering and some who couldn't care less. Selling by the street seemed like a tedious job. Though we weren't doing any hard physical labour and were simply squatting, the time spent waiting, looking and hoping for a customer, felt so tiring. Our hearts would beat faster when someone approached, then beat slower when they haggled over the price, then sink when they left without buying anything. I prayed for someone to buy them soon so that I could return to Nakul and check on him.

Months had passed since the bombing on my home. Perhaps, Nakul and I had grown a bit too. I could not tell. My saree had worn out and torn. Madam had given me a long piece of cloth which she had used as a sarong. I draped it like a saree. Under the Japanese rule, tensions between the Indians and Burmese seemed to have lessened, and I could see many Indians in the market.

'I think we'll have to eat these snails. Nobody seems to care for them. Come on, let's start cleaning them,' Madam said. She showed me how to scrape out the flesh. 'Pull, pierce, twist and turn.' While I did that, Madam kept calling out, 'Fresh snails! Very healthy. Full of nutrition. A small package filled with strength for your tired, exhausted bodies. Inexpensive, but rich.' A young man finally stopped by and had a closer look. Without much haggling, he pulled out two paper notes and paid.

'Did he pay a lot?' I asked excitedly.

'Not really a lot. Just what I asked for: two cents,' she replied.

'Just two cents? Aren't cents paid in coins?' I asked.

'They used to be. That was during British Raj. The Japanese government has issued new paper currency.

No more coins. Now, no matter how small the amount, it has a paper note,' she said. She handed me a note, which had designs along the border printed in red ink, the 'The Japanese Government' and 'One Cent' written on it.

'So, Burma is no longer under British rule but under the Japanese?' I asked.

'Yes. One foreign ruler has gone only to be replaced by another.'

We walked across the street and bought a little rice from a store run by an Indian. I noticed that Madam did not spend all the money. Perhaps she was saving for lean days like Ma–Baba used to.

'Didn't you say you wanted the Indians out along with the British?' I asked her on our way back. 'How come an Indian is running a store here?'

'I heard the Indians in Burma have teamed up with the Japanese, and the Japanese Empire is helping the Indians build an army to overthrow the British rule in India,' she said.

'I hope they do. I hope they drive the British away from India,' I replied.

With time, Nakul got better, and settled into a new routine. We would leave the hut early to pick snails, collect mushrooms under Madam's watchful eye, and, sometimes, hunt frogs. The farmer from the paddy field I had gone to with Madam had spotted me in the field and chased me away, running behind me with a stick, but I outran him into the forest. We avoided his land now. Instead, Madam taught us how to spot edible frogs in marshes and ponds. Madam went to sell our finds in town only every few days, never on two days in a row. 'People like these things only once in a while. If I take them every day, they will stop noticing me. They should think my wares are rare and wait for me,' she said. She preferred going alone on most days and took us along only when there was something heavy to carry or that had to be cleaned. If she returned in a good mood along with some rice, it meant she had done well. If not, it meant otherwise.

One evening, she returned with extra rice. 'Wow, did you sell everything at the market?' Nakul asked. Madam simply smiled. 'You can eat some today and save the rest for another day,' she said. How had she earned so much that day when she had carried only a basket of herbs to sell? Something didn't seem right to me.

The next morning, Madam left for the market again. She didn't return.

Nakul and I waited, looking for her silhouette now that the sun had started to set. But there was no crinkle of dry leaves under footsteps. Nakul and I kept getting up throughout the night to stand by the door of our hut and look for her, straining to hear her voice among the croaking of crickets and the howling of jackals. The next morning, we hoped we would find her in her hut, but it was empty. Her second set of clothes and her basket were also missing.

'She's gone,' I declared to Nakul.

'Should we go look for her?' he asked.

'Where would we look? We don't even know her name. We know nothing of her family. All we know is that she started living in the forest to avoid bombings,' I said.

'Could she have been attacked and taken away by the Japanese?' he asked.

'That *could* be. But she always kept out of the way of Japanese soldiers,' I said.

'Maybe she went back to her family.'

'Maybe. But the fact is that she's gone now.'

'What do you mean gone? Like how Ma–Baba are gone?' Nakul asked.

'No, not gone like that. I mean she's left here and gone to live somewhere else. She was saving up money, so I think she's been planning on leaving for a while,' I explained.

Nakul's eyebrows drew together. 'But how could she leave us?' Tears began welling up in his eyes.

'Why not? She wasn't family. She wasn't related to us. She made that clear when she asked us to call her Madam. And anyway'—I put my arm around Nakul's small shoulder—'we didn't like her that much, right? She could be quite scary. Now, we don't have to keep worrying about upsetting her,' I said.

'But it was nice to have a grown-up around. It felt safe, even if she was mad.' By now, the tears had started rolling down Nakul's cheeks.

Deep down, I felt the same as him, but I had to pretend I wasn't scared. 'I'm older than you. Think of me as a grown-up. I'll keep you safe,' I promised.

Chapter 8

CHEATS AND FAKES

We played hide-and-seek more often, now that we didn't have to worry about Madam yelling at us for wasting time or shouting too loudly when we found each other. However, I worried about keeping Nakul safe. I felt responsible for his safety.

The huts were close to crumbling down. The walls had cracks and the roof could fall off on the next stormy night. The limestone train had faded and the cow dung that Ma had smeared to smoothen the floor kept flaking off. Now there was just mud and gravel, which pricked our skin when we lay down.

Finding food became more difficult. Sometimes I took Nakul with me to look, but because he'd keep running off on his own, I'd have to keep an eye on him all the time. That's why I usually left him in the hut, or whatever was left of it. It was easier that way. 'I'll go get some food. You be quiet and hide here. Don't come out, no matter who calls out to you,' I'd tell him.

I'd always expect him to answer with, 'What if I peek a little? What if it's a kitten seeking shelter who calls out to me?' But he never did. He had stopped arguing with me, at least not as much as he used to around Ma–Baba.

One day, I stepped out of the hut to go look for food, but Nakul grabbed my wrist. 'Wait, Lakhmi. There's a mouse here. It comes every day after you leave and nibbles at my toes. Please, I'm scared.'

'It's just a tiny thing. You can just shout boo and scare it away into a hole,' I said.

'What about the crows and snakes that could come for it?' he said.

I knew about the mouse or rat or whatever it was. I still can't tell the difference between a mouse and a rat. But it was a small one. I wasn't scared of its nibbles or its predators. I was scared that once the hut completely fell apart, we would be like the mouse, having to live in a tiny hole, homeless and alone. How long would we be able to hide from the Japanese, who apparently took away children and girls to work, or some Burmese people, who disliked us Indians.

'May I please come with you?' Nakul asked.

'But I'm just going to get food. I won't be long.'

'I didn't like what you got yesterday. I'll help find something better.'

I knew Nakul had been craving rice. The previous day, I had only been able to boil some leaves to make a tasteless soup. On a lucky day, I would find a jackfruit in the forest that would last us two or three days, or sometimes wild plantains or papayas, if monkeys and elephants hadn't got there first.

'Please, take me along,' he begged.

'All right, but only if you do as I say,' I said.

We sneaked into the rice mill Madam had once taken us to. I hoped we could find some stray grains of rice. But the labourer on duty didn't let us anywhere near the chaff. 'No more sieving through chaff from now on,' he yelled.

'Please show me where you throw it. We'll go there,' I said.

'A shopkeeper took the last stock to be sold as cattle feed. Harvesting season is over. There's no chaff any more until the next season,' he said.

'It's okay, Lakhmi,' Nakul said, tugging at my hand. 'We can boil some leaves. Let's go.'

'I've promised to take care of you. I can't give up so easily,' I said. I led him to the fields to pick some snails and sell them in the market. But the fields had gone dry. It looked like even snails would be available only next season.

'Come on, let's go,' said Nakul.

'There's one last thing I can try,' I said. I took his hand and started walking towards the market in town.

Nakul realised immediately where I was taking him. 'Let's not walk to the market. It's too tiring. And there's no point. We don't have anything to sell or any money to buy something.'

I pulled out a five-rupee note from the waistband of my skirt and waved it at him.

'Oh!' His eyes lit up. 'So much money! Five rupees! That's a lot. Where did you get it?' he asked.

'Surprise, surprise!' I teased.

'Did you steal it?'

'No! I would never steal. Madam gave it to me the day before she left. She said it was for the work we did. She had a big bundle of these notes,' I said.

'Where did she get so much money from?'

'She said a wealthy customer who regularly bought medicinal herbs and snails from her gave it to her. He was grateful that her herbs saved his wife and gave her the money.'

'And she gave you five rupees from that stash? But you didn't bring it out till now even though we've been starving?'

'I've been saving it for an emergency,' I said. 'I thought if we came across a way to buy tickets to India, we could. But then we don't know anyone in India. We haven't met anyone in our families. We don't know where exactly Ma–Baba's homes are … or were.'

'Then why use the money now? Let's save it,' Nakul said.

'I don't want you to fall sick or lose your strength again. You haven't eaten properly in a long time. Let's buy some rice today and hide away the rest of the money.'

When we got to the shop, I cheerfully asked for some rice and handed over the five-rupee note. The Indian shopkeeper looked at me in disbelief, his eyes narrowing, and pulled the note from my hand. He held it up to the light and looked at it closely. Then he brought it up right up to his potato-like face and went through every picture and every letter printed on it.

'Where did you get this?' he finally asked angrily.

I was so shocked by his reaction that no words left my mouth. What had gone wrong?

'Tell me, where did you get this from?' he asked again.

'Madam gave it to her,' Nakul replied on my behalf.

'Who Madam? Where is she? What's her name?' the shopkeeper yelled. I noticed how red his mouth was from the paan he was chewing.

'We … we don't know,' I said. 'Just take the money, give us the rice and please return the change.'

He waved the note in my face. 'This money is worthless. It's fake. You cannot buy anything with this.'

'How can that be? Look here!' I pointed to the words on the note. 'It's the new currency issued by the Japanese government.'

'This is a counterfeit note. Look at the slit in the design on the back.'

'Maybe it's supposed to look like this. I don't see what's wrong with it!' I replied.

'The British and the Americans have been pushing these fake notes into Burma to make people lose faith in the Japanese money. When you cannot buy anything with the money you have, you'll stop trusting the Japanese government,' he said.

'But I've worked for this money. I've earned it!'

'That may be the case but you cannot buy anything with this. This is as good as trash,' he said. He put the note into the front pocket of his shirt.

'Then why did you keep it? Give it back to us,' I demanded.

'I can't do that. We've received orders that any counterfeit money we come across should be seized and handed over to the Japanese representatives,' he said.

'Please give it back. It's our money.' My throat was getting tighter. I felt tears stinging my eyes.

'We also have orders to hand over anyone who brings in fake money.' With that, he pushed us out.

A homeless man who was begging on the street outside the shop had seen what had happened. 'He's done you a favour,' he said to us. 'He could have handed you over to the Japanese. They're proving to be worse than the British.'

'Why did he need the note if it's fake?' Nakul asked.

'He'll probably give it to the Japanese and say that he was cheated by a customer and has suffered a loss. He might get compensated for the loss.'

'You mean he'll get an original five-rupee note if this is fake?' I asked.

'Probably,' the man replied.

'This is cheating!' Nakul turned towards the shop. 'You're a cheater!' he yelled. No one seemed to care, neither the shopkeeper nor the people walking by.

'No point making a spectacle. No one will believe two homeless kids in rags can possess five rupees. People will think you're circulating fake notes on behalf of the British and the Americans,' the man said.

'What do we do now, Lakhmi?' Nakul asked.

'I would have suggested begging, but I don't want competition here. I hardly make anything myself. People are less generous during war. Everyone is struggling. Maybe find a street with wealthy people and no beggars,' the man said.

'Should we do that, Lakhmi?' asked Nakul.

I pulled Nakul across the road and whispered sternly into his ears, 'No. Never, ever think of begging. It would have broken Ma–Baba's hearts. We've survived this long without begging, haven't we? We'll find a way. As for the money, fake or not, it's rightfully ours.'

'Are you going to fight the shopkeeper and get the money back?' Nakul asked.

'I'm going to get the rice,' I said firmly.

Chapter 9

A MARCH TO CHANGE

I climbed up a mango tree by the road to get a bird's-eye view. Then I positioned myself on a branch and remained well hidden amidst its leaves. No one could see me up there. The people in the market had all turned their attention to a sound that was growing louder. The sound of heavy boots. I quickly climbed down the tree, gestured Nakul to wait there and sneaked into the shop. The shopkeeper was outside on the street. I grabbed two heaps of rice and tied it up in the cloth I was carrying. But when I turned around, the shopkeeper was right there, his eyes filled with fire, his angry mouth still red from chewing paan. He was so big that he blocked my way out of the shop. I couldn't escape. Nakul was still under the tree across the road watching me with tears in his eyes. The sound of boots stomping was getting louder. I was sure the shopkeeper would hand me over to the military, the police, the Japanese—whoever it was that was marching. Dhap, dhap, dhap the boots sounded in unison. Dhak, dhak, dhak beat my heart. Then suddenly, we heard a tune, and words in Hindustani. They were singing a Hindustani song!

'Kadam kadam badhaye ja,
Khushi ke geet gaaye ja,
Yeh zindagi hai kom ki
Tu kom pe lutaye ja.'

The shopkeeper turned around and craned his neck to try and see who was singing. That was my chance to escape. I pushed him hard, but it only seemed like a nudge. Luckily for me, he tripped on a step, lost balance and went tumbling and rolling like a ball into the street. I sped away. I ran across the road and hid behind the trees with Nakul, listening to the song the whole time. It had been long since I had heard the music of our people.

'Lakhmi, see, look at them. They're women. Women soldiers.'

'What? No, Nakul.' I panted, trying to catch my breath. 'They're men. Women cannot be soldiers.'

'No, Lakhmi, see, see!'

Nakul was being stubborn again. You know how younger siblings can be. They think they're always right. Then they keep pestering you until you agree with them. 'See, see!' he said again.

I had been hiding my thin frame behind the large trunk of a tree. On Nakul's insistence, I peeped out from behind the tree. He was right. They were women! Dressed in khaki shirts and trousers that didn't have a single crease, and with a rifle in their hands, they marched ahead. The weight of the rifles didn't seem to bother them. They looked strong and proud. Their hair was either cut short or neatly braided. Not a strand was out of place. Heads held high, their arms and legs moved in sync. I didn't even hear anyone saying, 'Left, right, left, right.' All I could hear was them singing together, a different song now.

'Hum Bharat ki beti hai,
Ab utha chuki talwar,
Hum marne se nahi darti.
Nahi peeche paanv ko dharti,
Aage hi aage badhti.'

It was encouraging to hear the words, '*We are daughters of India. We have drawn out our swords. We are not afraid of death. We do not turn back. We march ahead.*'

I held Nakul's hand and followed the small marching group while singing along. People stopped and watched them with wide eyes and gaping mouths. I guess that's what they wanted. It must have been their way to inspire others to join them.

The marching stopped at the square and one of the soldiers stepped forward. She drew her sword and waved it in the air. 'Inquilab Zindabad!' she shouted. She looked about Ma's age. More people gathered around her.

'Isn't she Mrs Mehta of Pagoda Road?' whispered someone in Burmese.

'Yes, the Indian businessman's wife,' said someone else.

'She's Mrs Lilavati Chhaganlal Mehta. She now calls herself a freedom fighter. She has joined Netaji's Indian National Army,' explained an Indian man.

'What's got into her? Coming from such a wealthy family, she has decided to become a soldier? I heard she's donated her family jewels for the cause. What craziness!'

'Worse still, she has enlisted her own daughters, Rama and Neelam.'

'There they are. Right at the front. They're looking at their mother as if she's their commander and not the woman who gave birth to them. They're the first Indian-origin girls born in Burma to join Netaji's Azad Hind Fauj.'

'Girls in the army? Surprising. I don't think women are fighting anywhere else in the world.'

'Yes, they usually serve in wars only as nurses. Anything more than that is not for women.'

'I heard she has left her comfortable house and lives in a camp with her daughters and other women soldiers. No woman in her right mind does that,' remarked another bystander.

'Netaji has done the impossible,' commented one of the bystanders.

'What? Creating an army of women?' mocked another bystander.

'Yes, indeed. He had also formed a strong army of both men and women, which is all set to take on the British Army, and throw them out of India. Netaji's fauj will bring us freedom,' he replied.

The soldiers were chanting 'Chalo Dilli. Chalo Dilli,' and some voices in the crowd joined them: 'Chalo Dilli! Inquilab Zindabad!'

Mrs Mehta held her sword high and said in a booming voice, 'I know you're all wondering how women can fight in a war against the British, let alone fight at all. Let me remind you: only eighty-seven years ago, Rani Lakshmi Bai of Jhansi charged at the British with a sword, riding a horse and with her son strapped to her back. We are daughters of the same Bharat. If Rani Lakshmi Bai could do it, so can we. We are daughters of Ma Durga and Ma Kali. We are not afraid of laying our lives for our motherland. We are the soldiers of the Rani of Jhansi Regiment of Netaji Subhas Chandra Bose's Azad Hind Fauj—the Indian National Army. We will march ahead—onwards to Delhi to form the Azad Hind government.'

The other soldiers cried out, 'Chalo Dilli!'

Mrs Mehta continued, 'I appeal to you all to send your daughters to serve Bharat. Every daughter of Hindustan can become a Rani. She can become an avatar of Rani Lakshmi Bai of Jhansi and cause the British sleepless nights. We will defeat them and win back our motherland.'

Have you ever had that feeling where your chest swells with pride and there's so much energy inside you that you feel like you're buzzing like a bee? Mrs Mehta's speech woke something inside me. Memories of the day our house was bombed came rushing back to me all at once. I felt cheated. I felt betrayed. The British had brought my parents here and then abandoned us. Treated us like slaves. Used us and left us to die. For my parents, for Nakul, I had to do whatever I could to drive the British out of the land my parents spoke so fondly of: India.

And the Japanese had driven away the British from Burma, hadn't they? So the British were not unbeatable. I was sure that Netaji's army would chase out the goras from India in the same way. I wanted to be there. I wanted to play my part.

'Lakhmi, Lakhmi,' Nakul said, pulling at my hand. 'You're a girl! You should join and take me along with you.'

I smiled at Nakul. 'We'll both go to India and chase away the British. We'll return to our homeland, like Ma–Baba kept dreaming of.'

'Yes, yes, all that, but firstly, we'll get food. We'll get a house!' Nakul said, smiling widely. 'We can live in the camp, Lakhmi, please. I can't take living in that hole any more. And it's been so long since we got some good food. Please, Lakhmi. Join. Become a soldier.'

'Yes, even I'm tired of starving,' I thought, though I didn't say anything to Nakul and just ruffled his hair.

Mrs Mehta was still speaking. She was now telling everyone who could qualify as a Rani.

'Number one: you should be ethnically Indian.'

'Check. We are ethnically Indians, Lakhmi,' Nakul said.

'Number two: though married women are accepted, nursing mothers aren't.'

'Lakhmi, does that mean unmarried girls are accepted?' Nakul asked.

'Yes, check this too. I'm unmarried,' I replied.

'Number three: you need to get permission from your father or your husband.'

'Our father is dead, and you have no husband, Lakhmi. How do we meet this condition? Maybe I can pretend to be your husband,' said Nakul.

'Don't talk nonsense,' I snapped. 'You're too young to fool anyone with that.'

'Number four: you should have crossed your eighteenth birthday.'

Nakul gasped. 'No! You're thirteen or fourteen, Lakhmi. I don't even know exactly how old you are. But I know you're not eighteen. What do we do now?' Nakul sat down on the ground and began to sob. 'I don't want to go back to the hole we call home. Don't make us go back.'

I knew I had to find a way in. Lord Jagannath had shown me a way. The rest was up to me.

Chapter 10

THE FREE ARMY

We followed the soldiers to the outskirts of Rangoon. We were uncertain of them and kept a distance, wanting to first see where they go. The group entered a bamboo forest, and seemed to disappear behind the thicket of the bamboos. Nakul stopped in his tracks and held my hand tight and gestured with his palm to stop.

'Lakhmi, are you sure they're human?' asked Nakul.

'What do you mean?'

'They just disappeared. Plus, everyone knows women cannot be soldiers. Maybe they're ghosts.'

'They're not ghosts, silly. They looked real. Other people in the town saw them too,' I reasoned.

'Do you remember Ma telling us how there are different kinds of ghosts? Some are white and tall as trees. Some have twisted feet. Some are invisible, and some take human form. Maybe these are the ones who can shapeshift. Maybe they were killed in the bombings or by bullets and their spirits have shapeshifted to look like women. And now they want to punish the British by acting like soldiers.'

'Shh ... Quiet, Nakul. They've just entered the bamboo forest. They haven't vanished into thin air.'

We waited a few more minutes and then followed them into the forest. Bamboo plants had been cut and a path had been laid. The road turned and curved at various places until it reached an open field that was surrounded by a bamboo fence. A wooden gate opened to the compound. A wooden board at the entrance read: *Rani of Jhansi Regiment Training Camp*. It was not fortified like the British Army camps we had seen before the war. The camp did have guards though. The guards were spread throughout the periphery of the fence. At the gate, there were both men and women guards wearing khaki shirts, shorts and black shoes and socks, and were holding rifles. One of the men guards looked at us and gestured with his hand asking, 'What?'

I felt Nakul's fingers reach for mine. 'What if he shoots us, Lakhmi?' Nakul whispered.

'He won't. Why would he?' I replied, though my throat had gone dry and my knees were shaky.

We approached the guards, and I mumbled, 'We're here to join the Indian National Army.'

'Huh? What was that? Speak louder,' the soldier said gruffly. He was huge and had a large moustache that twisted over his cheeks.

'We-we're here to join the Rani of Jhansi Regiment!' I said loudly.

'Only women can join the Rani of Jhansi Regiment. Boys and children'—he pointed at Nakul—'cannot.'

'He can join Netaji's army, like you did,' I replied.

He snorted. 'This isn't some free-for-all place. We're looking for soldiers. We need warriors to fight. We don't need kids. Go back home.'

'But I want to be a soldier. I want to fight the British and free India,' said Nakul.

'I too want to join and fight like the women soldiers,' I said.

'For that, you need to be above eighteen. You look like you're hardly twelve and your brother doesn't even look like he is ten years old,' he snubbed.

'I'm not a child,' I declared.

He sighed. 'Even if I believe you're above eighteen, you look totally malnourished. You're too weak to be a soldier. Go on, off you go now!' he ordered.

We stood where we were, which made him even angrier. 'Leave! Now! Don't waste our time.'

He yelled so loudly that Nakul and I stumbled back in fright. Then we turned and walked back into the bamboo forest. Nakul was drained. He sat in the shade and closed his eyes. 'I'm too tired, Lakhmi. I cannot walk back. Let's just stay here.'

I marched back to the soldier. 'Please, could you at least give me some water? My brother is very thirsty and tired. He needs water.'

The guard immediately came with me and poured water into Nakul's mouth from his water bottle. Then he looked me straight in the eye and said, 'You need to go home now.'

It was already dark. There was no point walking back to the rubble we called home. It was too far away. We decided to stay in the bamboo forest. It was dark and quiet here too, like around the place we lived. Fireflies lit up the darkness.

'Lakhmi, I can hear my stomach go *gud-gud*. It's rumbling. I think it's going to start hurting, the way it did two days ago,' said Nakul.

'You're hungry,' I said. 'Wait here.' I looked for a piece of fresh bamboo. Fortunately, I found a cut piece of bamboo a few feet away. Someone must have left behind some pieces they didn't want. I filled the bamboo with the rice from my cloth sack and went searching for water. A little distance away from the Rani camp, in the bamboo forest was a small house. Some INA uniforms were hung out on a clothesline. That was perhaps the backyard, but there was no fence around the mud house. I took water from a drum outside with a metal mug kept next to it, and poured the water into the bamboo tube. I then covered the ends with fresh leaves. I spotted a piece of wood with some embers still on it, along with some charcoal. They looked like remnants of a bonfire lit for warmth. I collected some cold charcoal and picked a wood with embers on its one end. When I got back to Nakul, I blew with my mouth over the embers until the fire was lit again. I lit some dry leaves and twigs on fire and placed the pieces of charcoal on them and on the piece of wood. When the charcoal was red-hot, I lay the bamboo tube over it, until the outside of the bamboo turned black. I used two sticks to lift the bamboo off the coal, removed the leaves from either end of the tube and scooped the cooked rice out once it had cooled down a little. I fed Nakul and had some rice myself. It felt so filling and satisfying.

The day had been eventful. 'We didn't have the slightest idea that we would be spending the night here, did we, Nakul?' I asked.

There was no reply. 'Nakul?' I whispered. He had dozed off. We slept near the embers, the heat helping us beat the cold.

The next morning, we woke up to the sound of a loud horn playing a tune. We later learnt it was called a bugle. I had decided that we were not going anywhere else now. I was going to sit at the gates of the camp until they recruited us to be soldiers.

The guards on duty in the morning were different from the one we had met the previous day. I could tell them my story afresh and maybe they would let me join their army, I thought. But first, we needed to make a good impression. Nakul and I tip-toed to the drum of water I had found the night before. I filled the bamboo tube with water and then we hurried back. I poured a little water into my palm and washed Nakul's face. 'Hold your fingers up. Let me see the water droplets,' Nakul said. He looked at the brown water dripping from my fingertips and pulled a face. 'Chhee ... how dirty. It must be the dust from the rice mill.' I then wet his hair and tried to set it neatly. It had grown quite a bit and was matted. I wished I could cut it off.

'There isn't enough water for you to wet your hair,' he said, pulling at my braid. I unravelled my hair and tried to run my fingers through it, but it was so knotted that I couldn't get very far. I sprinkled a few drops of water on my head and braided my hair again. I remembered how Ma would comb my hair every day and oil it whenever she could afford some extra oil.

I brushed off the dust and dry leaves stuck to Nakul's shirt and shorts, and straightened my blouse and skirt.

'We look neat, don't we?' I asked Nakul.

Nakul held up his hand to his face and looked into an imaginary mirror, studying himself from different angles. 'Now no one can stop us from joining the army,' he said.

As we marched to the gate, copying the soldiers from the day before, he chanted, 'Ek, do, ek. Ek, do, ek. Left, right, left.' On reaching the gate, Nakul stopped with a loud stomp of his feet and said loudly, 'Thamb!'

The guards burst out laughing. 'Very good, very good,' they said.

'If I'm good, why not let me join the army like you?' Nakul asked.

'Well, fauj is not a game, little boy,' said one of the soldiers.

'See how fast I learnt? My sister and I are smart,' Nakul insisted.

'Yes, we've survived bombings and lived in jungles all alone. We will become excellent soldiers. Please give us a chance,' I pleaded. But the guards didn't listen. They simply shook their heads and gestured for us to leave.

We waited for the guards on duty to change again. 'Namaskar!' I greeted them with folded hands, and Nakul quickly joined his hands.

'Jai Hind,' the soldiers responded.

'We saw the soldiers march yesterday. I was surprised to see women soldiers. I couldn't believe my eyes. At first, we thought they were ghosts,' I said.

'Yes, we're ghosts. You should be scared of us and run back home, far from here. We can eat you alive,' one of them teased.

'We also want to be like you,' Nakul said.

'So, you want to become a ghost?' the soldier asked.

'Please don't talk to me like I'm a silly child. I know you're all real soldiers and not ghosts,' I said.

'All right then, let me talk to you like you're an adult and tell you why I agree we are ghosts. Where do you think ghosts are usually found?' he asked.

'In graveyards and cremation grounds. In abandoned houses,' I replied.

'War fields are large graveyards. When war strikes, it leaves not just abandoned houses but abandoned villages, towns and cities. We pass through them scarred, battered, carrying everyone's pain. Doesn't that make us ghosts?' He looked off into the distance for a moment. 'You're too young for this. Go home.'

'Leave and go back to your parents, kids. They're probably worried about you,' the other soldier said.

No matter how hard we tried to convince them, or how many trips we took to the gate, or how many different soldiers we approached, they all said no. Most of them said the same things too: 'We don't recruit children. You're too weak. You look much younger than you claim to be.'

It was evening, and Nakul was hungry again.

I hadn't gone looking for food. I had spent the entire day trying to convince the guards to let us in. The soldiers through the different shifts had all watched us, while we sat under a tree opposite the gate hoping that someone would let us in. The soldier who had spoken to us in the morning about being a ghost walked up to us. He crouched down and said softly, 'Why aren't you going home? This is no place for children.'

'We have no home,' I replied.

'The planes dropped bombs on our home,' Nakul added.

'The British left us here and later bombed our homes. They killed our parents. We want to fight the British and drive them away,' I said.

He led us to the front of the house we had seen last night. He went inside and got two boiled eggs for us. 'I am Lance Naik Yashpal Yadav,' he said.

'We are Laxmi and Nakul.' I replied. He smiled and nodded. Another soldier with beard and a turban stepped out and handed a bunch of bananas to us. Without uttering a word, we went aside and began preparing wood for a bonfire.

'Don't you stay inside the camp?' Nakul asked.

'We stay here. This house is our barrack. No male member is allowed inside the Rani camp. We only guard the outside. Only officers above the rank of Major and Netaji himself are allowed inside,' he said.

'Please tell us how we can join the war against the British,' I pleaded.

He sighed. 'I've seen war. I've been part of the British Indian Army for long. I saw bloodshed like I'd never seen before when the Japanese attacked Singapore and Britain surrendered. War isn't pretty at all. It's better to have children as far away from it as possible,' he said.

'If that's the case, then why are *you* still part of an army? Why didn't you just return home?' I asked.

'Well, we didn't have much choice. After being defeated by the Japanese in Singapore, the British handed all of us Indian soldiers to the Japanese and asked us to answer to their command. What are we, cattle? We were handed over from one command to another like we were sheep. We felt cheated. We're proud soldiers—we want to be treated like warriors even in defeat, not like slaves,' he said.

'Is that why you joined the INA?' I asked.

'When Singapore fell to Japanese forces, Britain surrendered and the British soldiers were taken as prisoners of war. Of the 85,000 prisoners of war, nearly 50,000 were Indian. Captain Mohan Singh, an Indian officer in the

British Army, addressed us Indian soldiers and urged us to join him in building an army that would free India from the British. He knew how unappreciated we felt under the British and how we didn't now want to be under the Japanese as prisoners. We wanted to be free from foreign rule. We had had enough,' he said.

The other soldier, who was lighting a fire now, added, 'We have been fighting other people's wars for too long. Now if we are to fight, it better be for our own motherland. Almost 45,000 Indian soldiers left the British Army to form a free army, the Azad Hind Fauj—the Indian National Army.'

'He is Sepoy Gobind Singh,' introduced Yadav.

Nakul, who usually got bored during stories filled with facts, was listening intently. 'Our parents worked for the British, building their railways. We feel cheated just like you,' Gobind Singh said.

'But, my dear boy, the reason we're telling you this is to show you that the Indian National Army is a professional army. We're all trained soldiers. It's not a village mela where anyone can walk in. Even volunteers without an army background have to go through rigorous training,' said Lance Naik Yashpal.

I knew I had to speak to someone else. 'Maybe Captain Mohan Singh will understand why we want to join the INA. Please let us meet him,' I asked.

'Captain Mohan Singh was a true soldier—a true professional. We would have been stricter with the induction of new soldiers,' he said.

'Is he here, inside the camp?' asked Nakul.

Yashpal ignored the question and began rearranging the firewood that was slipping down the bonfire. Gobind

Singh broke the silence, 'Mohan Singh had a disagreement with the Japanese, so they arrested him.'

'So, are you commanded by the Japanese? Did you come back under foreign rule?' I asked.

Yashpal's eyes twinkled, his smile stretching up to his ears. 'Six months later, Netaji arrived,' he said. 'He hid in a submarine and travelled from Germany to Singapore. On reaching Singapore, he took over the command of the Azad Hind Fauj. He thundered, "Chalo Dilli!" Through his speech, he inspired all the Indians listening to him. Indians in Singapore donated money and jewellery to help him in his fight for India's freedom. He is not only a good orator but also has a plan in place to raise resources and negotiate with the Japanese to fight this war. With him leading us, we believe we can defeat the mighty British crown.'

'So here we are, ready to lay our lives for our motherland,' Gobind Singh said. 'The British call us traitors and deserters, but we were traitors when we fought for England and swore allegiance to the British crown. Now we are freedom fighters. Our allegiance is to the land we were born in,' Yashpal added.

'We were born in Burma, but our parents were born in India. Our family has always dreamt of returning to our homeland. We too want to fight for the freedom of our motherland,' I said.

The two soldiers simply smiled and nodded.

Nakul and I returned to the bamboo grove. It was cold that evening and we were shivering. Yashpal and Gobind noticed us huddled together and brought us hot dal. 'Drink this and eat some rotis. You'll feel warmer,' Yashpal said. 'We're forbidden from inviting anyone other than our fellow soldiers into our barracks. I'm sorry you have to spend the night here,' Gobind said.

Nakul slurped the lentil soup from the bowl. When he put the bowl down, he had a yellow moustache. 'So delicious. It's been so long since we had some dal,' he said.

Though it wasn't as tasty as the one Ma made, it was filling and hot. I felt the warmth spread across my body.

'My little son used to get a moustache every time he drank milk, just like your dal moustache,' Yashpal said.

'How old is your son?' I asked.

'Well, he was about one when I saw him last. Now he too must have graduated to dal moustaches.' We laughed.

Gobind said, 'It's been nearly three years since we went home. We were deployed overseas in Malaya and Singapore. We haven't been able to return since the war broke. I wonder if we'll ever return.'

Yashpal added, 'We've made a choice. Netaji said, "Give me blood, and I shall give you freedom." We're ready to lay our lives down for freedom.'

Gobind stood up and pretended to adjust a microphone. '*Tum mujhe khoon do, mai tumhe aazadi doonga.*'

Nakul and I spent a second night in the bamboo grove, curled beside the fire the soldiers helped us light.

Chapter 11

ANOTHER LAKSHMI

The next morning, we woke to the sound of the bugle again. The sun had just risen above the horizon. A silhouette emerged: a figure on a horse rode out of the camp. I pictured Rani of Jhansi riding out. Only a baby strapped to the figure's back was missing. A few hours later, when the sun was up and bright, the rider returned on the horse. She looked so powerful in her khaki shirt, jodhpur trousers and riding shoes, a rifle strapped to her back. I wanted to become just like her.

'Who's that?' I asked Yashpal Yadav, who was back at the main gate on duty.

'She's the commander of the Rani of Jhansi Regiment, Captain Lakshmi Swaminathan,' he said.

Ma always said, 'Everything is destined. There are signs all around you. We have to spot them and follow these signs.' That day, I felt as though Ma were speaking to me through signs, trying to guide me towards my destiny. Did you spot the same sign I did? The regiment was named after Rani Lakshmi Bai of Jhansi. The first commander of this regiment was Captain Lakshmi. And I'm also Laxmi.

'Please let me meet Captain Lakshmi,' I pleaded.

'No' replied Yashpal. He was stern again now that he was on duty at the entry gate.

'Please! I think she may understand me and will let me join her. Please help me meet her,' I said. But Yashpal didn't budge.

Nakul brought his palms together, eyes shining with tears. 'Please help us. We've been waiting outside the gates for two days now. I keep thinking of Ma–Baba. If they were alive, we would not have had to wait like this outside the gates. They would have done the talking for us. They would have got us into the army. I miss Ma–Baba.' He wept.

Yahspal's face fell.

I jumped in, 'Please. We're beginning to lose hope.'

'Okay,' Yashpal finally said. 'I'll let you meet our INA officers who come as instructors to the Ranis. Wait here, both of you.'

It was a while before he came back out. 'Come in. Major Salim, the weapons instructor, will meet you,' he said and let us through. The gate opened into an open field with a large two-storeyed house in the middle, which was flanked by several small bamboo huts with thatched roofs. Closer to the gate and away from the main house, were a group of three huts. 'These are the offices,' pointed Yashpal.

I expected the officer to be shooting targets with a gun or training young soldiers, but he was sitting at a table and reading some papers and signing on them. He looked up at us when we walked in.

'Jai Hind, sir. These children want to join the Azad Hind Fauj. This young girl wants to be a Rani,' Yashpal said.

Major Salim shook his head nonchalantly and went back to looking at his papers.

'Please, just give us a chance. We too want to join the Azad Hind Fauj and drive away the British from India,' I urged.

He looked directly into my eyes and sternly said, 'To drive away the British from India, we will have to go to war with them. A real war. And war, dear child, is not for little kids.'

I held his gaze. 'But war has come to us anyway. Ma, Baba, Nakul and I were gladly living in our own world. The planes came from nowhere and dropped bombs on our home. There's no escape from war when the entire world is fighting. It's better to be brave and be part of the army and fight for a cause than die without having tried.'

I expected him to be impressed with my speech, maybe start clapping. Instead, he dismissed us with a wave of his hand. 'Take her away now,' he said to Yashpal.

'I promise I will....' But Yahspal led me away before I could continue to make my case.

I didn't feel like talking to the soldiers that night. I accepted the dal and rice they gave us only because of Nakul.

'There are many things that help build an army: discipline, obedience, adherence to rules. We had already broken the rules by taking you to meet the officer when we knew that children cannot be enlisted. The age-limit rule cannot be broken. We are bound to follow orders and couldn't let you stay in the office for longer. When on duty, we cannot be friendly,' said Yashpal.

'We wish we could do more for you, but our hands are tied,' Gobind said.

So, neither the soldiers at the gate nor the officers inside would help us. We had hit a wall.

After Nakul fell asleep, I lay awake and watched the stars, wondering what was actually destined for me. I had tried and failed to follow the signs. I wished Ma–Baba were with me. Tears flowed down my face. It had been a long time since I'd cried. Exhausted, I drifted into sleep, hoping to dream of Ma–Baba.

Chapter 12

BECOMING INDIRA

The third morning, we woke up again to the call of the bugle. I had hoped that I would have been inside by now, responding to the call and doing what the other Ranis do. That was not to be. 'Will we gain entry, Lakhmi?' Nakul asked, sitting up and rubbing his eyes. 'If not, what'll we do next?'

I dreaded this question—what next?— but I couldn't let Nakul know I was scared and disappointed. I had to make him think not joining wasn't a big deal. I remembered asking Ma–Baba if we could go off to India on a ship like the others. I don't think they had enough money for the fare, but Ma didn't say that. Instead, she said, 'A voyage by ship is one of the most unpleasant experiences. Passengers are tossed and thrown by the waves, their stomach churns and people vomit. By the time you reach the shore, you are drained and weak.'

I had to come up with something similar. 'We've been watching them for three days, but they haven't gone to fight anyone the whole time. They hardly come out. This army camp is like a prison! It's best we don't get in.'

'But they have food,' Nakul replied.

'The food isn't great. The dal they gave us yesterday was so watery and the rice grains so thick and hard. Let's leave.'

Nakul hadn't given up. 'Let me sleep a little more, Lakhmi, and dream a little more. I'm trying to see Ma–Baba and Ma's dalma in my mind.'

I knew I had to try one more time. This time, I'd let go of all my politeness.

'What if I change my approach?' I thought. I climbed a mango tree to get a good view. I was now looking over the walls of the camp. Something unusual caught my eye. I may not have known what the usual routine at the camp was, but I could sense that something was different today. Everyone was rushing around, with some people barking orders at others.

Whenever there's a break from the routine, people become tense and easily irritated. There's a sense of urgency in the air. People will run around, getting things done. And then there'll be one person who's so tense that they simply run around pretending to work. I used to see this happen whenever there was a big gora saheb that would come to visit and inspect the work on the railway lines. It was similar here.

Some Ranis were drawing lines with chalk powder on the ground, some were setting up chairs, a couple were setting up the dais. One Rani was all over the place, carrying a vase of wild flowers and chatting non-stop to the other Ranis, probably asking what needed to be done next. Another Rani was running around so much to finish things that she was creating a bigger mess for herself along the way. She crashed into the chairs, which fell down and had to be picked up. She then missed a step, tumbled down from the dais and crashed into a potted plant, which broke. Now, the mud and the broken pot had to be cleaned up. It was a bit funny watching the chaos, but it told me someone important was visiting.

I stayed up in the tree, waiting for signs of any new arrivals. Then, from a distance, I spotted a black motor car heading our way. I quickly slid down the tree trunk and rushed to the middle of the road, just in time to come face to face with the car and wave to stop it. The guards at the gate shouted, 'Get out! Get off the road!' I pretended not to hear and stood still. The car came to a screeching halt. I've always loved the sound of a screeching car. *Kee ... kee ... keech!* The driver, who was in INA uniform, immediately stepped out, absolutely fuming. 'Have you lost your mind? What's wrong with you? If I hadn't managed to stop the car, do you know what would have happened?' If this had been a magical story like the ones Ma would tell us, arrows of fire would have shot out from his eyes, turning me into ashes. The driver was so angry that I wondered for a moment if he really was going to shoot arrows at me, but just then, I heard a strong yet calm voice. 'This stunt that you pulled off could have got you killed. Yet, I am impressed with your courage.'

The man stepped out of the car. He wore khaki uniform, jodhpurs, a tilted cap and round glasses. He had no stars or stripes on his shoulders or on his arms. But he commanded respect and all. The soldiers who had gathered around us and also those at the gate stood at attention. 'Leave the child,' he ordered the guard who was holding me.

'Ji, Netaji,' the guard replied.

Oh! This was Netaji! The legendary Netaji! I puffed out my chest and yelled, 'Jai Hind, Netaji!' I had hoped the earth would shudder with my storming cry. Instead, I could hear muffled laughter from the soldiers. Netaji simply smiled and asked me, 'Why did you do this?'

'I want to join the Azad Hind Fauj,' I said. Nakul slowly made his way through the soldiers, came next to me and nervously held my arm.

When Netaji continued to look at me and Nakul without saying a word, I decided to add, 'None of them are letting me join. They say I am a child.'

'That you are, child,' he replied.

'Why can't children join hands to fight the British? After all, we have faced war and lost our parents to British bombs. We are victims of the British too, so why can't we fight them?' I asked.

'Well, there are rules, you see,' he said.

'Rules! Why are such rules even made? I thought the whole point of the Azad Hind Fauj was to kick out the British. I thought any Indians who are willing to fight for the cause are welcome. We're here to punish the British for what they did to our parents. We want to return to our motherland, just like the way my parents wanted to return to their village in the Orissa province. Why should the rules stop us?' I didn't care how I sounded. I didn't worry about whether I sounded impolite. This felt like my last chance. Netaji was the only one who could bend the rules. 'Here we are, two Indian children all alone in a foreign land with no family, no friends. Shouldn't our own army take us in?'

Netaji listened the whole time I spoke. Finally, he said, 'You certainly have the fire required in a soldier of Azad Hind. Join me.' He led me inside the camp and directed a soldier to take us to the office. Nakul stuck close to me, trying to hide himself in the folds of my saree pallu. We stepped into the same office that I had stepped into the previous day. It was a bamboo hut with a table and chair facing the door and few chairs neatly arranged around the table. After many months, we sat on chairs. We waited for a while. At one point, a girl with long braids peeped into the room but hurried off before I could ask her if she had come for us. Outside, Netaji was being greeted by the Ranis with firm 'Jai Hinds!' and crisp salutes. The Rani I had seen on horseback led the others.

Netaji and the Rani, followed by another officer, approached me, and Netaji asked, 'What's your name?'

'Laxmi. Laxmi Rath,' I replied.

'Oh! Laxmi. Meet the commander of the Rani of Jhansi Regiment, Captain Lakshmi Swaminathan.'

'Jai Hind,' we said to each other.

'Your name is Laxmi and your officer's name is also Lakshmi,' said Netaji with a smile. 'How can that be? We can't have two of you with the same name in the regiment. It'll lead to confusion.'

'You could call me what Ma called me—Lakhmi,' I replied.

'That still sounds a lot like Laxmi,' said Captain Lakshmi.

'I'll give you a new name,' said Netaji. 'From today on, you are a soldier. This regiment is your new family, and you'll have a new name to match. You are now Indira.'

'Indira,' I mumbled. The name sounded nice, but it felt so weird to think of myself as Indira. I can't say it instantly felt good.

Netaji placed his hand on Nakul's shoulder and asked his name. 'Nakul Rath,' he replied. 'That's a name that doesn't need to be changed,' he added. I thought it would have been nice if I too could retain my name like Nakul.

My feelings must have shown on my face, or maybe Netaji wanted me to feel at home, because he said, 'Did you know my roots are also in Orissa, just like yours?' I shook my head.

'I was born in Cuttack, the capital of Utkala, or Orissa Province, the same region your parents came from,' he said. 'I'm so happy to have a younger sister from close to my home join the Azad Hind Fauj.' Hearing this made me feel a little better. I felt like I had a guardian now, someone who had a connection to my parents' home. 'You are the first ever Rani from Odisha. We have soldiers in the Rani Regiment who come from families that are Punjabi, Tamil, Bangla, Awadhi ... but not from any Oriya family. I'm glad to have you join the Rani of Jhansi Regiment, dear Indira.'

I've often wondered why he chose to name me Indira. Perhaps it's because Indira is another name for Goddess Laxmi. Perhaps it was just a popular name back then. I later heard that even freedom fighter Jawaharlal Nehru's daughter was called Indira. Netaji respected the freedom fighters in India—he had named INA brigades after Gandhi, Nehru and Azad—though they didn't always agree with each other on *how* to get freedom.

While all this was going on, there was an officer in uniform, with many badges on his chest, who stood silently in the corner and watched. After Netaji left, he approached me.

'Why do you think Netaji has come here today?' he asked me.

'There's some kind of ceremony happening,' I replied.

'How do you know that?'

'I saw from atop a tree. Preparations were on.'

'What do you mean by preparations?'

'Chairs were being arranged. A dais was set up. The Ranis seemed tense and in a hurry. It seemed like an important person was visiting.'

'How did you know when Netaji would arrive?'

'Well, I didn't. I was up in the tree when I noticed a motor car coming, and I figured there must be someone important in there. I didn't know it would be Netaji.'

'You think well and are also not afraid of risking your life,' he said.

'How did you and your brother get by after your parents died?'

I told him about Madam and living in the woods. 'So you're a fighter and a survivor,' he said.

Nakul nudged me. 'I think that's you, Lakhmi.' I hadn't realised that Captain Lakshmi had been shouting, 'Indira, Indira' to call me. It was going to take some time for me to get used to my new name. I hurried out of the office with Nakul.

'Jai Hind, Indira. This is Rani Chandra. She'll show you your living quarters and explain your duties,' she said.

Rani Chandra was much older than the rest of us. She seemed even older than Ma. I held Nakul's hand to lead him along, but Captain Lakshmi said, 'Just you, Indira. Not your brother. This is a women's regiment. No male members are allowed to live here.' 'But I can't just leave my brother. He's a child,' I said, pulling him close.

Rani Chandra looked at us with kind eyes. 'You have us now. We're all one family. You'll live with the Rani of Jhansi Regiment and Nakul can live with the male soldiers of the Azad Hind Fauj,' she said.

Nakul gripped me. 'I-I don't want to stay away from you, L-lakhmi,' he said, choking on his tears.

'I don't either.' I turned to Rani Chandra and Captain Lakshmi. 'Can he please stay with me? Just for a while?'

'Rules cannot be broken, I'm afraid,' Rani Chandra said.

'He's never lived on his own. Maybe he can stay with me for only a few days,' I pleaded.

'This is why we don't allow nursing mothers and children. It's to avoid situations like this,' Captain Lakshmi said. 'When one rule is broken, there are demands for other rules to be bent as well. If you cannot follow the rules, you'll have to leave.'

Nakul and I looked at each other. We didn't want to be apart but we knew we had no home but a pile of rubble to go back to.

'My sons are also living in the Azad Hind Fauj camp,' said Rani Chandra. 'We get to meet on Sundays. You two can see each other every week.'

I hugged Nakul tightly, ruffled his hair and kissed the top of his head. 'Take care of yourself, Nakul. Eat well.'

He sobbed, gripping on to my skirt with his small hands. 'You take care too. Become a warrior and push the British out of India. Then we can return to the village Ma–Baba told us all those stories about.'

'I will, Nakul,' I said, my voice cracking. 'We'll go home together soon.'

Chapter 13

BOOTS AND BROOMS

New name, new home, new look—everything was changing. It felt good to take a warm bath after so much time. Rani Chandra handed me my clothes, the khaki uniform I had been dreaming of. I couldn't wait to see myself in the mirror. I was sure I looked like Captain Lakshmi on her horse. The mirror said something else, though. Have you ever seen those scarecrows that are just a bunch of sticks tied criss-cross without enough hay for stuffing? Some oversized clothes are thrown on them, and when the wind blows, they fill up like balloons and fly away. That's what I looked like.

'As a soldier, you should always be well-dressed. Your uniform is to be neat, clean and well-pressed,' said Rani Chandra.

'But I look funny. These clothes are too big and loose for me,' I mumbled.

'Maybe you're just too small,' she said. 'We don't have children's clothes.'

I couldn't argue with that.

'Come, let's find you a pair of shoes,' she said, adding, 'If they're big, you can stuff them with cotton or rags.' She tipped out black shoes from a sack. 'Some of these are smaller than I expected!' I exclaimed, and found a pair that fit me.

'These are shoes that once belonged to Gurkha soldiers of the British Army. When the Japanese captured the British camps, they handed over these uniforms and shoes.' She braided my hair. She handed me a backpack, a metal plate and mug, PT uniform and rolled bedding. 'This is all that you require here. Never lose your backpack and your belongings.'

I just had to alter my uniform with a few stitches and get a rifle in my hands. Then, I'd look like a real soldier. 'There's one last thing you need for your work. I'll be right back,' Rani Chandra said. The time had come. I was about to get my weapon.

She came back with something in her hands. 'A broom!' I said when I saw what it was. 'Really?'

'Yes. Your duty is to clean the room and the premises and to help me in the kitchen.'

'But I don't want to do that. I want to fight the British! I want to be a soldier,' I said.

'You're not ready for that. And soldiers need to eat and keep clean, don't they?'

'But why me? Why should *I* do this?'

'All the Ranis who are old, or ailing or unfit to go to war do these types of chores. You're unfit for war because you're too young, so you will have to help the older Ranis until you're ready,' she said.

Sweeping wasn't that bad, honestly. I went from room to room and hall to hall, crept under beds and looked behind cupboards. I gathered all the dust and garbage. Garbage, I found out, tells you a lot more than you'd think. It holds secrets.

I started discovering who secretly liked to eat what. Some corners had raw mangoes and salt hidden in them. Some spots had pickles. I even found a handkerchief full of sugar. That was a haul. During a war, a fistful of sugar is like hidden treasure. I didn't know that until I was asked to help in the kitchen.

Rani Chandra was the head of the kitchen. Rani Jayashree helped her by keeping an eye on the food supplies. Though one of the INA soldiers was the quarter master whose job it was to keep track of all the weapons, the ammunition and the rations, he was not allowed inside the camp, so Rani Jayashree took charge. Lying on her bed, propping herself up on her elbow like a reclining Buddha, she watched over everything that went in and out of the kitchen and pantry. Though she was old and suffered knee pain, which meant she was allowed a cot, she hardly missed a thing. Well, except maybe during those hot afternoons after lunch when she'd doze off.

My first day had one of those afternoons. Some sugar had been stolen. Our commander, Janaki Thevar, ordered everyone to gather in the hall. 'Is this a place for thieves? Is this how you think soldiers behave? Strength doesn't make anyone a true soldier, nor does plain courage. Even dacoits have strength and courage. It is integrity and character that set soldiers apart,' she thundered. 'Do not ever forget the principles of the Azad Hind Fauj and our Rani of Jhansi Regiment. What are they?'

All the Ranis spoke in unison. 'Ittefaq, etmad, kurbani!' I later learnt what that meant: unity, faith, sacrifice. These words were also on the badges the soldiers had pinned to their forage caps.

The assembled Ranis were standing in their companies. The regiment was divided into companies: Alpha, Bravo, Charlie and the Headquarter Company. These companies were divided into platoons and then sections. Trying to catch the thief by just asking wasn't going to work. No one would confess, especially since it wasn't just the thief who would be punished but the company too.

I looked around, wondering which company I would fit into. None of the company commanders looked at me invitingly. I felt lost and unwanted. Rani Chadra patted on my shoulder, walked up to Captain Thevar and whispered something into her ears. Captain Thevar glanced at me and nodded in agreement to something Rani Chandra was saying.

Rani Chandra addressed the companies and asked, 'Which company wants a new Rani?'

'Not us,' came the reply from everyone.

'Why? Why don't you want her?' Rani Chandra asked angrily.

'She's too young', 'She's too weak', 'She'll lag behind and pull the company down during all our competitions', 'She doesn't even look educated', 'She's dressed so shabbily.'

At the last comment, Captain Janaki Thevar turned to face me. 'This isn't acceptable,' she shouted. 'I want your uniform to be neatly ironed and well-fitted. I don't care how you do it, but get it done.' I shuddered, while she walked away as if screaming was nothing unusual.

'Don't worry. She just has a loud voice. That's her greatest strength. She commands over the Ranis and controls the regiment with the help of her booming scary voice,' whispered a girl leaning over my shoulder. She was slightly older than me and was standing behind me. I had seen her peeping into the office when I was waiting. I hadn't noticed her coming behind me. She may have perhaps sneaked in later than others. When I looked at the girl, she smiled. 'I'm Harpreet.'

'I'm Laxmi—wait, no. I'm Indira,' I replied. Maybe she would be my first friend.

'Harpreet!' yelled Captain Thevar. 'Aren't you supposed to be in your company? Why are you still chatting away with the new girl?'

Harpreet briskly walked towards her company and fell in line with her platoon. Captain Thevar continued, 'Now, you need to tell me who stole the sugar. Remember, we live together as a family. Taking something that belongs to all of us is unsoldierly.'

I was still standing around by myself like a lost goat without its herd.

'It could be the new girl. I saw her in the kitchen today,' said one Rani.

Blaming me was the easiest thing to do! No company would be punished if it was proven that I was the sugar thief.

'It wasn't me. I didn't do anything,' I mumbled.

'She first needs a company. Since she has been allotted the tasks of housekeeping and kitchen duties, I propose she should be in Headquarter Company,' said Rani Chandra to Captain Thevar.

That was how I ended up joining HQ Company, which mainly had soldiers in administrative and supporting tasks. I found myself in the company of most Ranis I had met during the day. Though they were older than me, it felt good to be with familiar faces.

'She's under my supervision today. It's her first day, and I don't think we should point a finger at her or anyone else without any evidence,' said Rani Chandra.

'I'm asking one last time. After this, I'll upturn your beds and look for the sugar myself,' said Captain Thevar. 'If you haven't eaten it all and I find it, you'll be severely punished.'

Well, if you remember, I had spotted some sugar in a handkerchief. I wondered what to do: Say something? Say nothing? Signal to Captain Thevar that I knew? Prove how wrong they all were to try and blame me?

'I know where the sugar is,' I whispered into Rani Chandra's ear. 'I saw it hidden in a kerchief while I was sweeping.'

'Shh ... We don't snitch on our compatriots,' she whispered back.

'But they were blaming me!' I said.

'That's another reason you shouldn't snitch. They will easily say that you stole it and hid it someone else's belongings. Or else, how would you know where to find it?'

'Right! No confession so I'm going to check everyone's belongings,' shouted Captain Thevar.

'No! Not again,' the Ranis shouted.

I found out later that the last time belongings were checked, many Ranis lost their secret stashes—including love letters from INA soldiers.

Rani Jayashree said, 'Captain, why not let a Rani investigate and find the culprit?'

Captain Thevar thought about this, looked at all the companies assembled and said, 'Okay, I already have too much on my plate. But, to investigate, we need someone neutral.'

'How about Indira?' asked Rani Chandra.

'Who Indira?'

'The new girl. She isn't friends with anyone yet and hasn't developed a connection with any of the companies. She's as neutral as you can get,' replied Rani Chandra.

'Yes, we can also assess if she has any detective skills,' Thevar joked, and the Ranis chuckled.

My first day was turning out more eventful than I had expected. I wondered how I would ever find the culprit. I knew where the sugar stash was. Maybe I could just hide and keep watch, and then catch the culprit red-handed. That would be easy.

'I'll do it' I declared.

Later, when everyone had left, I told Rani Chandra my plan. 'And how do you know that the sugar is kept there?' she asked.

'Because I saw it while cleaning,' I replied.

'So, do you go snooping around other people's things while cleaning? Why would you do that? You were asked to find the sugar thief, only a little while ago. While you cleaned in the morning, you weren't tasked with finding the thief.' she said.

I was baffled. 'I didn't snoop! I was being attentive and alert. And I was just doing my job.'

'Then let's just prove you were being attentive and alert. Declaring that you already know where the sugar is will make people accuse you.'

'So, what do I do?'

'Get proof and use your logic to figure out who did it.'

'But it's my first day. I know nothing about the camp and the routine.'

'Hmm, fair enough.' Rani Chandra paused for a moment. 'Rani Emily will help you and tell you about the workings of the camp,' she said and led me to the kitchen.

Emily Rosamma was almost as thin as me but slightly taller. She had braided hair and neatly folded the braids. I later learnt that she had recently turned eighteen.

Emily stuttered and stammered for a while before managing to string some words together in Hindustani: '*Aapko kya maloom hai?*'

I looked at her puzzled. 'Huh?'

Irritated, she mumbled something in a different language, and then retorted, 'What do you know?'

'Nothing,' I replied.

She struggled again with her next sentence. All the soldiers were expected to speak only in Hindustani. Emily was still learning it.

'I can help you only if you tell the truth' she said.

'I found the sugar hidden in a handkerchief while I was cleaning the rooms.'

'Barracks,' she corrected me.

'But this camp is within a huge compound of a house, and many Ranis sleep inside the house. I don't think barracks are like these,' I said.

'But here, they expect us to learn all the military lingo, as well as Hindustani, you see,' she said.

'What language do you speak at home? Where are you from?' I asked.

'We speak Tamil. I've come from Malaya. My grandparents migrated from India in search of work. We all worked at the rubber plantations run by the British,' she said.

'Same with my parents. They came from India to Burma in a steamer to lay railway lines for the British. I've never been to India.'

Emily smiled. 'I too have never been there. But I've heard many stories of India from my grandmother. When she was ill, she believed that if she made a pilgrimage to the church of Vailankanni Mata, she would be healed. But she never travelled back to India.'

'I feel you. My father told us how majestic and magical Bhagwaan Jagannath's temple in Puri is. It's right by the sea.'

'The Vailankanni church is also by the sea. Do you think they're close by?'

Rani Jayashree, who always sat by the kitchen door keeping account of rations, must have overheard us. 'India has very long coastlines on both the east and the west. They span thousands of kilometres. Both the shrines you mentioned are on the east coast, but far away from each other,' she said.

'Is India as big as Burma?' I asked.

'It's much, much bigger,' Jayashree replied.

'Bigger than Malaya and Singapore together?' asked Emily.

'Bigger. Bigger than Malaya, Singapore, Thailand and Burma together.'

'Oh! Really? How do you know?' I asked.

'You'll also learn these things when you attend your classes. Emily, you need to pay more attention in Hindustani class,' Jayashree said.

Emily ignored the remark and turned to me. 'So, tell me, what else do you know about the sugar thief?'

'Nothing else. I simply know where the stolen sugar is hidden. That's it. I know nothing beyond that.'

'Then what's the problem? Case solved. Show me where exactly you found it and we'll figure out whom it belongs to.'

'I don't want people to think I went snooping around and checking their belongings in their absence, even before I was entrusted with the task to find the thief. I don't want the Ranis to distrust and dislike me.'

'We'll handle that. First show me where you found it.'

I took Emily across the hall towards the other wing of the house and stealthily pointed to a bundle of clothes tied in an old dupatta at the other end of the large room. 'There was a handkerchief full of sugar shoved in there. It fell out when I lifted the bundle to sweep under it. I quickly put it back.' Now, a girl sat next to the bundle, clutching it guardingly. We could only see her back and her long braids in the faint candlelight.

'Very soon, everyone will assemble for dinner in the hall. We can see who she is then. Until then, let's keep watch.'

The bell rang and many Ranis stood up. The girl turned around. It was Harpreet! The girl who had spoken to me kindly, the one I thought would become my first friend. I spotted her but in the chaos of all the Ranis rushing at the sound of the bell, Emily had missed her.

We both ran to the dining hall for our duties. I served rice while Emily served dal to the Ranis who came for dinner. They all waited in line with their plates and mugs. We made a mental note of the Ranis with long, braided hair. There were nearly thirty of them.

'Did you notice any grains of sugar on anyone's mouth or hands?' I asked Emily. I liked Harpreet, and thought she could be my friend, and so didn't want to reveal she was the thief.

'Don't you think they would have cleaned themselves up before assembling here?' she asked.

She was right. I tried a different approach. 'Emily, was there any time yesterday when no one was present inside the kitchen or inside the house?'

'Yes, when Netaji addressed us. We had all assembled outside and were preparing together.'

'While I was stuck in the office, being interviewed by a scary officer. He asked me so many questions and cross-questions. I don't know what he wanted to find out,' I complained.

That's when I remembered a girl with long braids peeping into the office while I waited with Nakul. It had been Harpreet! How had I not recognised her earlier?

I thought of Nakul. Had he eaten well? Were the others being kind to him? Was he missing me? I was waiting to see him on Sunday.

Emily gave me a nudge. 'So how do you think we should go about catching the sugar thief?'

'I'm not sure,' I mumbled. 'Maybe we can figure it out tomorrow.'

Chapter 14

SHARP EYES, SMART TURNOUT

The Ranis of my platoon, including Emily and me, were to sleep in a bamboo hut outside the main house. The main house had some platoons. The Ranis who were officers lived in the first floor of the house.

Though Rani Jayashree was given a cot, everyone else slept on the floor. They had all changed onto their regular personal clothes. Some wore sarees, some long skirts and some salwar kameez. I watched Emily open her bedding roll on the floor and followed suit. The roll opened into thick canvas sheet on which the soldiers lied down.

'Place your uniform under the sheet and then sleep over it,' said Emily. 'Captain Thevar doesn't like any creases. The iron box is available only at noon and in the evenings before dinner. There's always a queue for it and you have to refill the coal in it if needed.'

'The uniform doesn't fit me well, so it's going to look shabby anyway,' I said.

Emily reached into her backpack and handed me a needle and some thread. 'Fix it then,' she said.

Straining under the lantern light, I tried to pass the thread through the eye of the needle. I missed the first time. I screwed my eyes up in concentration before trying again.

'Another misfire!' Emily said, laughing. 'Target missed.'

On the third attempt, I got it. 'Bullseye!' cried Emily.

I jumped up and looked around in panic. 'What? Where's the bull?' One charge from a bull and this bamboo shack would crumble down.

The Ranis fell about laughing, rolling on the floor, clutching their stomachs.

'You have a lot to learn, little one,' Rani Jayashree finally said. 'Military lingo, reading and writing Hindustani, firing, bayonet training, grenade handling. You need to be battle ready.'

I interrupted her, partly because I didn't want her to continue lecturing me and partly because I felt hopeful and excited. 'That means I will learn how to fire a rifle and things that will make me a soldier.'

'Yes, Netaji is particular about the training of all Ranis. Even the Ranis who serve as nurses need to train in warfare.'

'That means I won't always be just sweeping and mopping! I'll be able to hold a gun!'

'Yes, when the time comes,' she assured me. 'Now, dear Rani Sharp Eyes, take this.' She handed me a small, rusted tin box filled with thread rolls. She took my uniform from me and used her forefinger to measure how much to be folded.

She reminded me of Ma. I had wanted to wear her sarees, so she had altered her old blouses for me in the same way. I remember the stitches she taught me. The running stitch was just like me running in the fields. The needle poked in and out, in and out, just like my feet would touch the ground and then spring up.

I couldn't see what stitch Rani Jayashree was using, but her fingers and the thread moved fast, and in no time, she handed my shirt and trousers to me. Emily helped me place them under my bedding to iron out the creases.

I hoped to wake up at the call of the bugle. Instead, I was shaken awake by Emily. 'Wake up, wake up. It's time.'

'But the bugle hasn't blown yet,' I argued. I looked around, rubbing my eyes. The entire company was up. 'Why is everyone awake? Is everything all right?'

'How do you think the person who blows the bugle wakes up? Some people have to wake up earlier than others,' she said.

'And me too?'

'Kitchen duty calls before the bugle call.'

We washed up and Emily told me we had to change into our PT uniforms—khaki shorts and white buttoned shirts. Before sunrise, we were in the kitchen, chopping, cutting, kneading and rolling chapatis.

The bugler and the drill team, dressed in their crisp uniforms, marched to hoist the flag sharp at 6 a.m. The saffron, white and green INA flag with the leaping tiger in the middle looked majestic fluttering against the rising sun. 'Stop walking around. Drop your spoon. Stand still,' Emily said. As the bugle blew, we all stood at attention. When the bugle stopped, the drill commands were given and everyone went back to their tasks. They all looked like dolls who restarted their movements after the key was wound.

'Today, everyone will be served tea without sugar,' announced Rani Chandra.

'No!' cried Emily.

'We get limited rations. Everything is measured as per authorisation of every soldier,' said Rani Chandra.

'What does that mean?' I asked.

'For instance, each soldier is entitled for say, 20 grams of dal, 50 grams of rice, 1 egg, 30 grams of vegetable, 2 grams of sugar and so on in a day. These are just examples; the Quarter Master knows the exact authorisation of every soldier. The entitled ration is then calculated for all soldiers and procured,' she explained. She paused momentarily, looked at the floor and thought for a while and continued, 'We are dependent on the Japanese for our rations and supplies. During war, things like sugar are a luxury. Since one of us stole some sugar, we all have to pay by having sugarless tea today.'

'Indira, how far are we with finding the sugar thief?' asked Rani Jayashree.

Emily chimed in, 'We're at it. We'll have the thief soon, won't we, Indira?' I simply nodded, wondering if I had to rat out Harpreet. If I gave her up, she would never want to be my friend.

'Okay, girls, time for your PT,' announced Rani Jayashree.

'Come on! Let's go. We don't want to be late and be shouted at by the PT ustad,' Emily said, pulling at my arm.

'Wait, I have to do something first,' I said.

Emily gave me a confused look but then said, 'Can't wait for you. Can't be late,' rushing out of the kitchen.

I walked to the wing I'd found the bundle of clothes in. Harpreet was there, alone, dressed and ready to leave for PT.

'Jai Hind,' I said to her.

'Jai Hind, new girl!' she replied. 'What are you doing here? Let's go for PT.'

'I wanted to speak to you.'

'Now? We'll be late. Trust me, no one wants to be late for PT.'

'It's urgent. I need to speak to you now, when we're alone.'

She raised her eyebrows. 'Okay, be quick about it.'

'I … I … I know you stole the sugar!' I said. Harpreet's face began turning red. 'I won't tell anyone, but you need to return it.'

Harpreet stood silent, not saying a word.

'Please, if you still have the sugar, give it to me. I'll sneak into the kitchen and leave it there. Nobody has to know it was you.'

'H-how do you know?' she finally said, stumbling over her words.

'It doesn't matter.'

'What if I deny it?'

'Well, today's tea will be served without sugar, so all the Ranis will be up against whoever stole it. Even the senior Ranis will be angry. They won't drop it, so I'll have to give you up. If you return it quietly, nobody will find out,' I said.

She looked down at the floor. 'I've eaten some, but there's a bit left,' she said. She bent down to look through the cloth bundle and then handed over the handkerchief of sugar. 'Don't ever be late for PT,' she added. I rushed back to the kitchen and quietly left the sugar by the huge tea pan and ran towards the PT parade ground.

All the Ranis had fallen in line and stood at attention. Captain Lakshmi was taking the morning report from all the company commanders. Harpreet had managed to sneak into line. I tried to do the same thing, but a tall, thin man who looked like a bamboo stick yelled, 'Stop!' So this was the PT ustad. He signalled for me to go back. I didn't know where to go. 'Harpreet, you too. I saw you joining late,' he shouted.

Harpreet jogged towards the end of the ground, so I followed her. I spotted dozens of backpacks all lined up. The PT ustad shouted from across the field, 'Pick up a bag and strap it to your back.'

I picked one up and almost toppled over. 'It's so heavy. What's inside? Stones?' I asked Harpreet.

'No, sand,' she replied, casually strapping a rucksack to her back. I used all my strength to heave the bag up and put my arms through the straps. Then I followed Harpreet as she ran along the boundary of the ground. I understood why no one wanted to be late for PT.

One round. Two rounds. Three rounds. I was beginning to feel giddy. 'How many more rounds do we need to take? I'm going to fall,' I panted.

'Don't speak. He'll only increase the number of rounds. Keep running until he asks us to stop,' she said over her shoulder.

I was seconds away from falling on my face when the PT ustad shouted, '*Stop. Murga ban jao.*' I knew what that meant. Ma would punish Nakul like this. 'Become a rooster' is a very popular punishment that Indian parents dole out to kids. Harpreet and I sat on our haunches, tucked our elbows behind our knees and held our ears with our fingers. He walked over to us and ordered, 'Stay in this position.'

'This is better than running with that load,' I muttered to Harpreet when he left to train the other Ranis.

'It's Ulfat Ustad's way of giving us some rest but making it look like a punishment. He likes to act tough,' she said.

After a while, when the PT parade moved to the other end of the ground, I asked softly, 'Why did you steal the sugar? It's not like sugar will help you when you're hungry.'

'For times like these,' she snapped. 'If we had some sugar to throw in our mouth now, we would instantly get energy.'

'Stealing is wrong,' I said, but the memory of taking rice for Nakul from that shop came to mind. We were starving, I told myself, and the shopkeeper was unfair. I only took what was rightfully ours. I couldn't let my brother die of hunger.

'You shouldn't have done it,' I told Harpreet. 'Rani Jayashree was furious. The Japanese give us limited sugar.'

'I know, but I was also angry. I wanted to have something nice to eat for once. I was tired of the same rice, dal, sabzi and occasional egg.'

'Isn't that what everyone eats in the camp?' I asked.

'Yes, what everyone is *supposed* to eat, though that doesn't always happen.'

'What do you mean?'

'All the Ranis from rich households have food brought for them from their homes, especially the ones whose families are nearby. They even get to go home on Sundays. Isn't that unfair?'

I didn't tell her that I was looking forward to meeting Nakul on Sunday. If Ma–Baba had still been around, I too would have gone home on Sundays.

'I agree. Everyone should get the same treatment,' I said.

'There are the Ranis from rich and influential families, and us, whom they address as estate girls.'

'What do you mean by estate girls?' I asked.

'Most of us worked as farm hands at estates run by the British. They treated us very badly. We were glad when the Japanese defeated them and took control of Burma. But then we realised the Japanese weren't much kinder. We wanted to return to our motherland. Then we heard Netaji's call to join him and drive the British away from India so that we could return home.'

The bell rang, signalling the end of forty-five minutes of physical training. With the thought of retuning to an India ruled by Indians, all my pain and complaints seemed like a small price to pay.

Breakfast was served at 7.30 a.m. That meant Emily Rosamma and I had to rush from the PT ground to help serve chapatis and tea.

Rani Jayashree smiled when she saw us. 'The sugar was returned with only a few spoonfuls missing,' she said.

'Returned!' exclaimed Emily. 'Oh no! How? When?'

'Isn't it a good thing that it was returned? We no longer have to find the thief,' I said.

'But this was a good chance for us to prove something and get out of housekeeping and kitchen chores. We could have shown everyone our skills and joined a fighting platoon,' she said.

For a minute, I wished I had known this earlier. I so badly wanted to learn to fight. The kitchen and housekeeping work looked easy, but it was so tiring. We woke up before the others, we had physical training like them and then we rushed back to set up service before they came for breakfast. At 8.30 a.m., we went with everyone else for drill parade. While the others were free at about 11 a.m. to attend to their personal chores, we were back cooking lunch. After lunch, while the rest got some time off or took a short nap, we attended to our personal affairs like bathing and washing and ironing our clothes. Then there were classes. My favourite class was Hindustani, the official language used in the INA. It was a mix of Hindi and Urdu, written in the English alphabet.

It was funny at first, learning A, B, C for Hindustani, since we usually used these letters for English. We practised spelling words like 'hum, tum, mai, aap'. These words seem easy but spelling them was tough! Emily Rosamma picked up Hindustani faster than the other Tamil-speaking girls. She often argued, 'Why should there be a "u" in "hum" and not an "a"? Why can't "aap" have a single "a"?' It was all fun until test days came around. That's when our ustad had fun punishing us.

All our instructors were ex-soldiers of the British Army who had heard Netaji's call and joined the INA. They were tough on us when it came to training and discipline, just like they were with the male soldiers. It was good to be treated like we were equal to men. Rosamma felt otherwise. 'I heard them say women cannot be as good as men,' she told me once. She thought our tough treatment was to break us and prove that we weren't as strong as the men. Well, that never happened. If Rani Lakshmi Bai could ride a horse and fight on the battlefield, why couldn't we, we Ranis believed.

After the flag was lowered at sunset and the bugle played again, we all had a break before dinner at 7 p.m. It was the same as lunch, though I found out later that we'd sometimes get an egg or a piece of fish. Before bedtime, the girls gathered outside the house and performed dances, sang songs, put up plays or played instruments. I was asked to go up on the verandah, which doubled up as a stage. It was my first time. I didn't know what to do. I just stood there, saluted and belted out, 'Jai Hind!' Nobody reacted. They were waiting for more, a song or a dance. I wasn't ready for either. I knew I had to do something fast or I'd be a laughing stock.

'Umm … I'm Laxmi,' I muttered. 'Now I'm Indira too. So I'm Laxmi Indira. I'm proud to be a Rani, a warrior for my motherland. "Jai Hind" is my favourite phrase. Every time I say it, my heart swells with pride. It makes me feel close to home. I speak many languages: Oriya, Hindi, English, Nepali, Burmese and I'm learning Tamil here. In all these languages, Jai Hind has the same effect on me. So let's say it one more time: Jai Hind!' All the Ranis shouted back, 'Jai Hind!'

Rani Chandra came up to me later. 'I've never heard such a passionate Jai Hind. I got goosebumps listening to you, Indira. I've heard it said hundreds of times but never the way you said it. Jai Hind, Indira.'

Chapter 15

SISTERS AND BROTHERS

No matter where in the world you are, there is something special about Sundays. You never need a calendar to remind you what day of the week it is. It's just the way the day starts—you immediately know it's a Sunday. It was going to be a relatively free day. I didn't have to hurry from the kitchen to the PT ground. I didn't have to hustle, run and jump around doing exercises only to run back to the kitchen. But what was most exciting was that I was going to see Nakul.

'Quick. Finish your work fast, girls. We need to catch the bus to the INA camp,' ordered Rani Jayashree. She had promised me that she would take me along.

I found myself kneading the dough faster and harder. 'Wait, wait. Don't throw the dough around like a stone. We have to eat that,' Rani Chandra cautioned.

Emily laughed. 'She's hitting the dough as though she's washing clothes at the dhobi ghat. *Dhap, dhap, dhap*.'

I blushed. I had wanted to finish early and rush to see Nakul. But the others were doing things slower than usual. While usually, their rolling pins rolled out the dough balls like they were shaking them awake, that Sunday their hands moved like they were giving the dough balls a relaxing massage. Being new and the youngest, I couldn't ask them to hurry up, but I could go faster with my chores.

'Shall I knead the dough for the rotis for lunch now?' I asked.

'Let's finish the rotis for breakfast now,' said Emily.

'But I have to go. I have to catch the bus,' I said.

'Don't worry about lunch. No rotis on Sundays. We will make khichdi. Just mix the lentils, potatoes and rice. If we're lucky enough to get spices, which is rare, we'll throw in a few masalas and call it biryani. That's Sunday lunch,' said Rani Jayashree. 'We need some rest too. The others have Sunday totally off, no parades, no training and no classes. But the stomach doesn't take a day off, so those of us with kitchen duties are always working.'

'Shall I quickly sweep and mop then?' I asked.

'No need. No sweeping on Sundays,' she chuckled. But then he spotted someone outside and called out, 'Sanda, why are you here on a Sunday?' she asked a girl in Burmese attire cutting grass. 'The grass doesn't know its Sunday. It grows every day and can be cut on Sundays too,' she joked. 'I need to work on all days to feed my family,' she added.

'Okay, Okay,' Rani Jayashree hurriedly replied.

Breakfast was served, and preparations for lunch began. While washing the rice, I wondered what time it was. I was scared I'd miss the bus. 'Leave everything now,

Indira. We have to go,' ordered Rani Chandra. 'The others will complete your duties.'

'Are you sure?' I didn't want to be punished later for a task that I was halfway through.

'Yes, I'm sure,' she said. 'One more thing we learn in the army is that we are a team. Away from our homes, we are a family. We need to stand by and support each other, not only in our professional tasks but also in our personal lives. Brotherhood among soldiers makes a strong army. As for the Rani regiment, we have something that makes us even stronger and more closely knit than the male soldiers of the INA—sisterhood.'

'Sisterhood isn't built only through serving together. We may now be fighting the same battle against the British, but even before we came together, we were fighting the same battles in our lives: fighting against patriarchy, against unfair traditions, against forced marriages, against everything that makes women feel small. We understand each other better because we've all been through similar things,' said Rani Jayashree.

Rani Chandra and I rushed to the bus stop inside the camp. I had expected a nice, comfortable bus, but there was a truck waiting for us. Rani Chandra stepped on one of the tyres, gripped a rope ranging from the steel frame over the cargo bed and climbed into the back of the truck. 'Come on. Get in,' she said, stretching her arm out for me.

I held on to her hand, placed my foot on the tyre and looked up. 'Wait, wait! I need a minute,' I said to her, jumping down. I had spotted a tree filled with bora berries. 'Nakul loves these berries. Let me get a few for him. They make him happy.' I ran to the tree.

'Be careful. The branches are thorny, so you may get pricked,' Rani Chandra warned me. I shook a branch that was hanging low with all my might, sending berries raining down. I filled my pockets with the bright red berries. 'What a great invention these pockets are!' I remarked.

'If only we had pockets in sarees and skirts too,' said one of the Ranis in the back of the truck.

'Men have pockets in their trousers, shorts—even their shirts! Didn't I tell you, Indira, that we women have fought many battles together?' said Rani Chandra.

The truck filled up with more Ranis. On weekdays, the truck took the Ranis serving as nurses to the INA hospital and brought them back every evening. On Sundays, it took the Ranis into town or the INA camp. Some Ranis preferred to cycle. This Sunday, Harpreet and three other Ranis were riding their bicycles into town. 'Bye! Have a great time!' they yelled and waved as we passed by.

The INA camp was bigger than the Rani Regiment camp. There were far more soldiers here. Rani Chandra led me to the meeting area, a big open ground. Two lanky young men in khaki INA uniforms waved at her and walked towards us. 'My sons, Kiran and Prakash,' she said to me. They were among those who hadn't been part of the British Army but had volunteered to join the Azad Hind Fauj.

'Help Indira find her little brother,' Rani Chandra told her sons. 'He's about ten years old.'

'That new little boy? Chotu? He's usually peering out of the fence near the doorway. He waits there every day,' said one of them. He pointed to a bamboo fence not far from us. There was Nakul, looking through the gaps in the fence, leaning forward against the slit bamboos.

'Nakul! Nakku!' I called out.

He turned around, startled. 'Lakhmi!' he yelled, and ran towards me.

He crashed into me so hard that I almost fell over. 'I've been waiting for you for so many days!' he said, throwing his arms around me. I wrapped my arms around him and lifted him off the ground. I wanted to swing him around, but he felt a little heavier than I remembered him being.

'How long have you been waiting at the fence?' I said, stroking his face. There were creases on his cheeks because he'd been pressing his face against the bamboo.

'Since morning. I've been waiting here every day,' he replied, plonking on the sand under a tree.

'But we can only meet on Sundays, remember? I'll be here at this time every Sunday,' I promised, sitting next to him.

'I miss you, Lakhmi. I miss Ma–Baba. I miss our home.' He pressed himself against me, trying to hide his tears. 'I miss us.'

'I'm here now, aren't I? Tell me, did you eat anything today? How's the food?' I asked.

'Three meals daily!' His eyes sparkled. 'I get rice and dal every day. Sometimes eggs and fish too.'

'So, you like it here?'

'No. There's no one to tell me stories. Everyone is so much older. They don't talk to me the way you and Ma did. Only big-man voices here,' he complained.

'You'll become like them, ready to fight the British,' I said.

'I don't know. So far, all I do is attend Hindustani class, run up and down to pass messages from one office to another. They call me a runner,' he replied.

'That sounds easy.'

'But I have to wake up so early! Here, everyone wakes up before the sun rises.'

'I have to wake up early too. I don't mind that so much, but I don't like the rush that follows. Run to the kitchen. Run to the PT ground. Run back to the kitchen. Run to class. Too much running,' I said.

I handed him the bora berries I'd brought along. 'My favourite!' he said. He chewed them one by one and spat the seeds out. 'I hope these seeds grow into trees. Then I'll get lots more berries.'

I told him all about the Rani camp, the people I met there, the friends I made, my duties.

'The routine at your Rani camp is the same as here. You also have PT, training, theory classes and evening games. The meal timings, even the food menu is the same. It's like there's no difference between men and women soldiers,' he said, looking surprised.

'Why would there be any difference?' I asked.

'No, no, just that we had never heard of women soldiers before. I thought maybe women soldiers would have it easier.' He looked at me apologetically.

'Netaji says that we are all soldiers. Men and women soldiers are equal and have to perform the same duties. In fact, when our forces enter India, he wants women soldiers to lead the march to Delhi,' I said.

'He said that? I figured many of the women are nurses and doctors, not fighters.'

'Even the Ranis who serve as nurses and doctors undergo weapons training. They'd also be able to fight if a war breaks out,' I said.

'I see many Ranis nursing unwell people at the hospital here. I thought you would come with them. That's why I waited here every day, hoping to see you. Can't you be a nurse so that I can meet you every day?' he said.

'That's not in my hands. I'm still learning the basics.' Nakul placed his head on my shoulder. 'And anyway, Nakul, we shouldn't forget that we joined the Azad Hind Fauj to throw the British out of India, to return home.'

Nakul nodded, his head still on my shoulder.

'For that, we have to forget about what we want for some time,' I said. 'We need to focus on learning and training. Then we'll be the best soldiers we can be. We need to make Ma–Baba proud. Remember, they're watching over us.' I pointed to the sky.

'I know. It's just that I wish there was somebody here with me. Someone I could talk to and trouble, the way I bug you,' he replied.

I hadn't noticed Rani Chandra walking up to us. 'You can talk to these two. They're your elder brothers, Kiran Dada and Prakash Dada,' she said.

'We'll look after him, Ma,' said Kiran.

'Don't worry about him. I'll teach him how to box and kick,' said Prakash, picking Nakul up and holding him up in the air.

Nakul burst into a fit of giggles while Rani Chandra's sons played with him. I felt relieved—finally it wasn't just me looking out for Nakul.

When we got back to the Rani camp, we were all ordered to line up for roll call before the flag was pulled down for the day. We stood in our platoons and companies, and the commanders checked off our names against the list to make sure everyone was there.

'Rani Chandra? Rani Nirmala? Rani Emily Rosamma? Rani Indira?' called out Rani Jayashree. She then marched up to Captain Thevar and said, 'All present. All okay.'

The other platoon commanders did the same. But when it was Rani Pritam's turn, she said, 'Three Ranis haven't returned yet.'

'It's sundown. It's an hour past curfew. How is it that they haven't returned yet?' barked Captain Thevar.

Rani Pritam stood at attention; her chin held high. 'That's the price of being a leader. You may not always be congratulated when all goes well. But if anything goes wrong, you'll have to face the fire even if it's not your fault,' Rani Chandra whispered. 'That's why I keep away from any command positions.'

'Who are the girls?' Captain Thevar demanded.

'Rani Annapurna, Rani Manjula and Rani Harshdeep,' Rani Pritam answered.

Those were the girls we'd seen cycling into town. I remembered Harpreet being with them too. I quickly turned towards her platoon and there she was, standing at the back in the last row.

'Did they get permission to go out? Where did they say they were going?' Captain Thevar asked.

'They said they were going to Rani Manjula's house in town and would return post lunch,' Rani Pritam replied. 'They might be on their way back now.'

Why was Rani Pritam not saying anything about Harpreet. Didn't she know they had all gone together?

'We saw Harpreet with them in the morning,' I whispered to Emily. 'She's here while the others aren't. Why is Rani Pritam not reporting that?'

'It's better to report three girls missing than to say one is back after leaving behind her three buddies. It looks bad for the company. I'm sure Pritam will deal with Harpreet on her own.'

Captain Thevar paced up and down, her eyes narrowed. 'Get the search parties ready,' she finally said. 'We'll have to go look for them.'

As Rani Pritam marched back to her platoon, we heard the squeaking of bicycles. Three meek voices said, 'Jai Hind.'

You could almost see the smoke coming out Captain Thevar's ears. 'Meet me in my office ... now!' she ordered. We learnt the next day that the three Ranis were made to run around the parade ground while carrying their bicycles and were forbidden from going out for the next two Sundays.

That night, while I was returning to my barrack after cleaning the kitchen, I noticed someone crawling in through a gap in the fence. Emily and I went closer to get a better look.

'Harpreet! What are you doing?' I asked.

'Shh ... quiet. Help me,' she said, pushing her bicycle in through the hole in a dilapidated part of the fence. 'Pull it in. Gently! Don't make so much noise.'

Emily and I tugged at the bicycle to get it in, and Harpreet followed. 'What's going on, Harpreet?' Emily snapped.

'Nothing! We were late getting back. So, I left my bicycle outside and crawled in to join everyone in line. The other three were scared to leave their bicycles outside. They thought they'd get stolen.'

'How could you leave them and come inside by yourself?' I asked.

'*I* didn't leave them. *They* left me! I told them to leave their bicycles outside and get in through the fence. We would have been here during roll call and could have got cycles later. But they left me to take the longer route through the main gate along with their bikes,' she said.

'Why were you late? Where did you go? *Really* go? Don't lie and say lunch at Manjula's house,' Emily said crossly.

Harpreet smiled mischievously. 'To the market in town. To a waterfall in the jungle. For a picnic. It could have been anything, but I won't tell.'

'I'm sure going off course was your idea,' Emily said to her.

'The four of you had fun and broke the rules. But while the three of them are punished, you're not. That's unfair,' I added.

'It's not my fault if they weren't smart enough to do what I did. Besides, it doesn't matter what rules you break. The only thing that matters is not getting caught,' Harpreet said.

'Is there any other rule you've made for yourself that you want to share with us?' Emily asked.

'Always show up where you're expected. Like today—we were expected to be present for roll call. No matter what, I showed up,' she said.

'Harpreet, not everyone is blind to your antics,' Emily said. 'Someday, you'll get caught. Every day can't be your lucky day.'

Chapter 16

BIRDS AT NIGHT

The day Emily predicted came. Harpreet was caught red-handed. She literally had her hand inside the sugar jar when Rani Jayashree nabbed her. 'You think if I'm unwell and sleepy, I can't see? My eyes are always watching,' she said.

Well, that's what we *think* she said. Emily told me, and someone else told her. All the Ranis were at their classes, and I was cleaning the rooms at the time. The story goes that Harpreet tried her best to twist and turn and break free. But Rani Jayashree, despite her joint pain, didn't let go. She twisted Harpreet's arm behind her back, and Harpreet had to kneel in pain. Rani Jayashree forced opened Harpreet's mouth. And just like Yashoda saw the universe in Lord Krishna's mouth, Rani Jayashree saw the INA flag flying high on Indian soil inside Harpreet's mouth. I don't know if that last bit is true, but that's what one of the Ranis said.

We heard that Harpreet tried to reason with Rani Jayashree. 'Why should I be punished? Why can't I have a little extra sugar?'

When Jayashree said that the sugar had to be shared with everybody and she couldn't have extra since we were all equal, Harpreet said, 'If that's the case, why do some girls get food from their homes? Their servants carry food for them. Their uniforms are stitched by their family tailors. Isn't that unfair?'

Though I still don't know for sure if that's exactly what Harpreet said, this was an issue the 'estate girl' and I talked about. Maybe Netaji had spies among us, or maybe it was simply that the officers reported everything to him. Anyway, that evening, it was announced that Ranis could no longer get food from their homes. We all had to eat the camp food.

Harpreet was punished for stealing. She had to spend an entire twenty-four hours without food in the lock-up, which was in the most guarded place in the camp, the Quarter Guard. The armoury, the treasury, the flag was all located in the structure that was the Quarter Guard.

After dinner, Captain Thevar reminded us of the three principles of the INA: ittefaq, etmad, kurbani. Unity, faith, sacrifice, along with a long lecture in her booming voice.

That evening, the Ranis in my barrack stayed up whispering and talking in bed. Rani Jayashree shouted, 'Stop this gupshup-gipshup. You girls yap, talk and giggle all day and all night. Off to sleep now.'

Emily always knew how to draw Rani Jayashree into the conversation. 'Did you hear Ponnamma is going to be an officer?

'Yes, I met her this evening. I'm very proud of her. We all are,' Rani Jayashree said. 'Now go to sleep.'

Emily ignored her request. 'How can she become an officer? She's not from a wealthy family. She's like us.'

'What do you mean?'

'I've noticed only Ranis from well-to-do families become officers. So, I didn't think estate girls could climb the ranks.'

'No, no, no! We're all equal. Netaji is very particular that every Rani should be treated equally and trained professionally. The only things you have to have to become an officer is an education—at least eight years of school and should know Hindi and English.'

'Oh, that's why! Most of the Ranis from estates and plantations haven't been to school or had to leave midway,' I said.

'The Ranis from well-off families have attended school and are educated. That's just privilege or, as we call it, destiny,' said Emily.

'Maybe when things get better and we're back in India, you girls can complete your studies and become officers. Free India will be the first country to have women fighters in its army,' said Jayashree.

'Did Ponnamma go to school and study for many years?' I asked.

'She did. She studied to become a teacher. Then her parents arranged her marriage. She heard Netaji's speech and it stirred something in her. So, she joined the Rani regiment to free India and to escape her arranged marriage. Her parents were furious. It took a lot of convincing before she got their permission. Now, she'll be among the first women army officers of free India. She chose her destiny. So have you all,' said Rani Jayashree. 'Okay, enough talking. Blow out the lamp and go to sleep.'

We blew out the kerosene lamp and waited silently to hear Rani Jayashree snore. It started after a few minutes.

*Zzz ... grrr ... brr ...*Emily held a crow feather up to Rani Jayashree's nose. She simply rubbed her nose and turned over, deep asleep. 'Now! Let's go,' whispered Emily, and we sneaked out.

I had hidden some chapatis for Harpreet. 'She must not have eaten enough,' I said.

'Yes, plus she's always hungry. I don't like her that much, Indira. I'm doing this just because she's your friend,' said Emily.

We tiptoed out of the hut towards the Quarter Guard. It was a pucca room with mud walls and clay tiles on the roof. The door was locked from the outside and a Rani was guarding the area. We crept towards the back, where the slanting roof was at its lowest. We held on to the wooden frame of the window, placed our feet on the uneven mud walls and climbed up. Halfway through, we caught hold of the wooden beam of the roof, and with its support got on to the roof. When on the roof, we had to be careful to place our feet between two clay tiles gently. A little excessive pressure could crack the tiles, and the sound might alert the sentries on duty. We gently pulled out a few tiles and looked into the lock up. Harpreet was lying on her back. Her eyes met ours. She smiled broadly.

'She's not even embarrassed about being locked up,' said Emily. Harpreet knew how to have fun no matter the situation. She was like a naughty kid who's made to stand outside the classroom as punishment but throws pebbles at passers-by instead of sulking. We tied the food package to a rope that we had carried and lowered it into the room. Harpreet opened the banana leaf package and said, 'Rotis! Did you not get parathas?'

Emily burst out, 'You don't deserve even this! You could simply say thank you. How ungrateful.'

Harpreet loved to see Emily riled up. 'Who'd rejoice at the sight of sukhi roti, Rosamma?' she said. 'You work in the kitchen. You could have secretly made some parathas for me.'

'That's it! I'm leaving. I don't want to get caught because of you. Why would I risk anything for an ungrateful person like you?' As Emily moved to leave, she accidently pushed a tile down.

'Who's there?' called out the sentry. Emily put a finger to her lips, signalling for me to keep quiet. We both lay there silently, trying hard to blend in with the tiles. Thankfully, we were on the back slope of the roof. Emily and I lay on our backs, looking up at the sky, waiting. Suddenly, the chirping of the crickets was interrupted by a familiar sound. One that shook me to my bones.

Scenes from the day Ma–Baba left us flashed before me. My heart pounded, and my chest felt tight. Was it the same sound? Or was I imagining it?

'Emily, can you hear that?' I asked.

'Yes. It's faint, but I think it's growing louder. What is that?'

I sat up. 'They're approaching! Planes! Bombers! Take cover,' I yelled.

'We are under attack,' yelled the guard. 'Bombers are approaching. All lights out! Take cover.' The Ranis began waking up in a panic. Everyone knew the drill for an aerial attack. Some Ranis quickly jumped out and ducked into the trenches.

The fighter planes were obviously faster than us. The first one dropped a bomb on the right wing of the main house. Luckily, the wing had already been almost entirely evacuated, but the fire quickly spread through the wooden beams. Rani Reena, who was on the first floor, fell through the floor when it gave way. She hit her head and lay on the ground. Rani Pema quickly dragged Reena out, saving her. Even though Reena and Pema weren't friends and came from totally different places, one risked her life for the other, all because of the promise we'd made to fight for India's freedom. That night made everyone's commitment and friendship even stronger.

Emily and I had slid down, picked the key hung in the Quarter Guard and freed Harpreet. As we ran towards the trenches, Harpreet screamed, 'The armoury!' We rushed back to save our rifles and ammunition. Some Ranis were already there, gathering the weapons. I strapped a rifle over each shoulder and grabbed two more in my hands. Emily and Harpreet did the same and together they carried a heavy box of ammunition. We ran back to the trenches.

Right after we got to safety, a second bomber followed and hit the armoury. The explosion was huge, shooting flames into the sky. We secretly wished those flames would reach up and grab the planes. We spent that night in the trenches, huddled together, many of us in pain, bleeding, with broken limbs, yet alert and ready to fight. The Ranis who were trained as nurses got to work. As trained, they had rushed out with the kits. They cleaned and stitched wounds and tied bandages, comforting us the whole time.

That night felt endless. I thought of when our home had been bombed and the night that followed. That had felt even longer because I'd been all alone. Sure, Nakul had been with me, but he was so young. The responsibility of being his only family had weighed me down. At the camp, I had found sisterhood, a family that took care of each other. After all, I was a child too—I wanted to be taken care of. I cried, not because of the attack but because I missed Ma–Baba so terribly. I wished I had come to Netaji sooner to become a soldier.

That night, it hit me: the enemy had noticed us. We were prepared for an aerial attack. We were told by our officers that the Americans and the British would target Japanese and INA bases in Burma. Though the Allied Forces included many other countries,

That's why we had dug the trenches around the camp and practiced the drill of what was to be done. Now, that it happened, the truth hit hard.

'It is proven that we were a threat to them. They don't consider us just a bunch of novice women. We are a threat to the mighty British and Americans,' remarked Rani Jayashree proudly while moaning in pain. She had broken her leg while jumping into the trench. I couldn't see her in the darkness but could only hear her, but I could sense pride in her voice.

'The fact that we had been hit by American planes had proved that not just the British but the Allied Forces too, which included the Americans and the French and many other countries, know about the Rani of Jhansi Regiment,' said Rani Chandra. 'However, only the British and Americans are deployed on the Burma front,' she added.

'Nah. Nah. I am the one they have taken notice of. They wanted to eliminate me. See, how accurately they targeted the Quarter Guard on the night I was locked in,' joked Harpreet and the Ranis burst into laughter.

Harpreet's joke made me wonder about the accuracy with which they targeted the camp. I arrived at a conclusion but held myself for saying it out loud. There was a mole among us. Somebody had passed on the exact location of key points of our camp.

Chapter 17

A SIGHTING

The next morning, we left the camp, or what remained of it. Emily, Harpreet and some others went into the burnt-down house and huts one last time. Emily scavenged through her belongings and could only find few burnt pages of her Bible. Harpreet found just a piece of an old family photograph. A broken bangle, the ashes of a letter, shards of the sugar jar Rani Jayashree protected, the charred tyres of the cycles Harpreet's friends had ridden—these were the remains.

One question played on loop in my mind: Who was the mole, the traitor?

We left the camp on horse-drawn carriages, bullock carts and a couple of lorries. The land next to the INA camp had been allotted to us. The male INA soldiers helped us set up tents. A makeshift hospital was created where the injured Ranis were treated.

The best thing was having Netaji visit us. He greeted every Rani by name, placed his hand on our heads, comforted us and praised our bravery. When it was my turn, he said, 'You look strong, Indira. It seems like it's time for you to join the fighting force.' My heart did somersaults in my chest. I couldn't believe it. I was finally going to be fighting soldier.

Setting up the new camp wasn't easy. Everything had to be built from scratch.

Amidst the commotion, I picked out a familiar voice. 'Lakhmi! Lakhmi!' I spotted Nakul. 'Have you seen Lakhmi? I mean, Indira?' He looked taller, more like a grown-up in his uniform. When he saw me, he rushed over, saying again and again, 'Thank God you're safe, thank God you're safe.'

He seemed settled in the INA camp, and was not as nervous and anxious like the first time I met him in the camp.

'Did they change your name as well?' I asked.

'Not really, but they call me Chotu.'

I ruffled his hair, happy to see him tall and well-fed.

'The two dadas you introduced me to, Kiran Da and Prakash Da—they always have my back,' he said.

'See? I knew they'd take care of you,' I said.

'I was so worried about you. I'm happy you're unhurt,' he said. 'I need to rush back to the office. There could be messages that I need to run and pass. I'll try to meet you in my next break.' We hugged, and he began walking away, only to suddenly stop in his tracks and turn around. 'Lakhmi, I think I saw Madam the other day, perhaps over a week ago.'

'Madam? You mean the madam whose name we never knew?' I asked.

'Yes. I'm not sure but I think I saw her outside the camp.'

'What do you mean you're not sure?'

'There was a woman outside the camp selling snacks. Jhalmuri and berries and stuff. She looked like Madam. I saw her from a distance, through the fence.'

'Did she recognise you?' I asked.

'No, I told you, I was so far away. I don't think she got a clear look at me.'

'Does she come every day? Is she here today?'

'I saw her just that one day. The guards asked her to move. They didn't let her sit outside the gate. After she left, I heard the duty officer shouting and ordering a soldier to burn the papers she left behind,' Nakul said.

'What papers?' I asked.

'The ones she used to wrap the jhalmuri in.'

'And what exactly did the officer shout?'

'Oh, the same kind of thing they always shout when there's a mistake. "Can't you think? Have you left your brain at home? If you see a sweet-talking woman, you easily believe her?" He went on and on.'

'He didn't say anything else?' I asked.

'You know how these officers scream brainlessly. The best thing is not to listen at all. Kiran Dada showed me how they go, "Blah, blah, koo, ki, aa, oh, blah, blah." All this nonsense at the top of their lungs. Then they calm down a bit and start making some sense. Only then do we have to listen carefully. They'll say, you better do this and that. And that's the order. Are the Rani officers the same?'

I smiled. 'They are. I think all officers are trained to be like that. Anyway, you mentioned some papers she left behind. Do you know what was written on them? Was there any yelling about that?'

'Yeah, the officer yelled, "How could you be so stupid? Do you not think at all? Paper is not easily available or cheap. Street hawkers use leaves, not paper. Now burn them all." See how first he said blah, blah, koo, ki and then the order came at the end? The only thing the officer actually had to say was "burn the papers".'

'Yes, that makes sense,' I replied.

Nakul looked smug. 'I told you. Kiran Dada is always right.'

'I mean, it makes sense to wonder why a street hawker would use expensive paper instead of leaves. Madam always used large leaves to wrap her stuff.'

'Oh, I remember,' Nakul replied. 'We wove the leaves into cones for berries and pulled out fibres from the banana trees to use as string to tie herbs.'

'Are you sure it was her?' I asked again.

'Oh, I don't know. The woman looked like her, but maybe it wasn't. I'm not even sure if she used the paper to wrap anything. Maybe she used leaves. But when she was leaving, she left a bundle of papers near the gate.'

'Something doesn't add up. Madam never told us her name. Why would anyone who lives with you hide her name from you? And she kept us in a hut away from hers. And then she simply vanished one morning without a trace,' I said.

'*And* she left us fake money, remember?' Nakul added.

'There was something fishy about her,' I said.

'Not just fishy. Slimy and froggy too!' Nakul laughed.

'She *did* help us, though,' I reminded him.

He stopped laughing and nodded solemnly. 'That's true, she did, she did. She taught us a lot of things. She was good sometimes—but sometimes, she was very bad,' he said. Nakul's eyebrows suddenly shot up. 'Oh! I forgot about everything while talking to you and now I'm late. I have to rush!' With that, he ran off.

I couldn't get Madam out of my mind. The more I thought of her, the more questions I had. She had appeared in our lives twice, and both times had been around a bombing.

Chapter 18

MOLES AND CLUES

We all worked towards setting up our new camp for the next few days. We first dug ditches around the boundary of the land. In case there was another attack, we could take cover in these trenches. 'Three feet deep and two feet wide. Enough to get inside and hide,' sang Emily.

'Imagine we all sleep here every night side by side. We'll look like a train line,' Harpreet said, laughing.

'My favourite memories are from when I was small and lived along the railway lines,' I said. I didn't mind the hard work of digging or setting up the camp. It all meant being closer to Nakul.

Our next task was building our barracks. So many Ranis had worked in plantations and estates, so this wasn't difficult. We cut bamboo, shaved down timber, knitted palm leaves, cut hay for the roofs and dug the earth. Our hands seemed to move in sync to the songs we sang.

'Kadam, kadam badhaye ja,
Khushi ke geet gaye ja.
Yeh zindagi hai kom ki,
Tu kom pe lutaye ja.'

One morning, I was called to the office. Inside was the same officer who had questioned me on my first day. I had learnt how to read ranks by looking at a uniform and by now, I had learnt his name. He was Colonel Shaukat Ali Malik. 'You've done a good job passing on information to me. I can see you're a keen observer. Yet you've missed something important,' he said.

Yes, I was a mole too. A mole for Netaji within the Rani camp.

Let me explain. A couple of days after my meeting with him on my first day, I had a second meeting with Colonel Malik. This time, Rani Chandra escorted me to the office and introduced me to Colonel Malik. After she left, he said, 'Rani Chandra has handpicked you from among all the Ranis. From our conversation at our first meeting, I would say I agree with Rani Chandra that you are trustworthy and can be entrusted with responsibilities.'

'I already have the responsibility of cooking and cleaning. What other responsibilities are you giving me?' I asked.

'I want you to continue cleaning and cooking diligently and carry on with whatever tasks are assigned to you. While doing your routine work and training, I need you to be alert and notice the goings-on around you, and will tell me everything that happens inside here. You will be my informant,' he said.

'What do you mean?' I'd asked.

'At first, tell me everything that you notice: the routine, what the Ranis talk about, what they do.'

'Is that it?' I asked.

'Once you are well-acquainted with the routine, you will be able to notice if there is anything unusual or anyone does anything unusual. That has to be reported to me,' he said.

I had been passing on information through a soldier who visited the Rani camp every day to deliver letters and notes between the two camps. Every time he came, he made a point to visit the kitchen for some water or a bite. He was a smooth talker, charming everyone, even the eagle-eyed Rani Jayashree. 'Amma Jayashree, you are truly a Rani. See, you're the only one with a throne, the only one who stretches her legs and sits and rules over this kitchen empire,' he once said. 'Enroute, I met a babaji who has been travelling the Himalayas. He got this *jadi-booti*. He said this herb can cure your joint pain.' Jayashree would offer him water and a roti for having travelled the distance on his horse in such a humid weather. 'Only this Rani has the power to gift me some sugar, nobody else,' he'd say to get some precious sugar with his roti.

Somewhere around this time, I would tell him if there was anything of importance. Our shot exchanges would sometimes be near the well in the backyard when I went to fill up some water for cooking, or sometimes while washing the utensils outside, or sometimes just in the kitchen when the other Ranis were busy with other chores or classes, and also when I visited the INA camp to see Nakul.

The soldier seemed to talk to most Ranis. I sometimes wondered if he came to only talk to me, or were there more informants like me among the Ranis. Initially, it was just the daily routine that I'd fill him in on. Then one day he said, 'The Hawk says now that you have understood the routine, tell us if you see anything suspicious.'

'What do you mean "suspicious"? I asked.

'Look out for someone noting details, making maps or going in and out frequently,' he said.

I had passed on anything that seemed remotely suspicious to me. I had even informed about the broken fence that Harpreet used to get in at odd times. I had also passed on info about any new visitor to the Rani camp.

After weeks of being an informant, here I was speaking to Colonel Malik a few days after the bombing. I had certainly missed something.

'What important thing have I missed?' I asked sheepishly looking around his office in the INA camp, which was similar to the one in Rani camp, but with maps on the walls. A metal almirah stood at the corner with a large 'X' drawn on in. The corners of the 'X' touched each corner of the almirah. In bold letters, 'In case of fire, move first,' was written on it. I made a mental note of all that I saw. Perhaps, I was nervous and so was looking around to distract myself. I was expecting Colonel Malik to chide me for I may have missed noticing a suspicious person in the Rani camp.

He instead calmly and sternly said, 'Somebody passed on all the details of the camp—the exact location of the barracks, the armoury, everything. If we had any intel earlier, the damage could have been averted. This is clearly an intelligence failure.'

I was sure of the loyalty of the Ranis. 'I think it's an outsider,' I said immediately.

'First rule of intelligence: trust no one but win everyone's trust. Understand, Rani Indira?'

'They all trust me,' I replied.

'Yes, they do. What's not to trust? You are the youngest, you obey them, you do the menial jobs, you are weak. Owing to your age, they underestimate you. Some even think you are naïve and foolish.'

'Do you too think I am foolish?' I asked hoping he wouldn't say 'yes'.

'No, you're not. In making them underestimate you, you're fooling them. That's good work, Indira.'

'Thank you,' I muttered.

He rubbed the sides of his head, his eyes closed. 'Yet, you've failed. You need to think back and figure out who the mole is. In the meantime, you may begin your combat training. You're dismissed.'

I should have saluted and marched out, but I stood there, my mind racing.

'Is there anything else, Indira?' he asked.

'Aah … hmm …'

'What is it? Tell me,' he demanded.

'I'm not sure, but I may have a suspect,' I said, my heart pounding in my chest.

'All right. Let's begin with the name.'

'I don't know her name.'

He raised his eyebrows. 'Go on. What is it that you do know?'

'I met her for the first time the day my house was bombed. Then she disappeared. Now, my brother saw her, only a few days before the Rani camp was bombed.' I told him all about the time we'd spent with Madam and what Nakul has seen outside the INA camp. He didn't seem surprised. It seemed like he already knew about Madam being sighted.

'Yes, I heard about it. She seems like a strong suspect, this Madam,' he said.

Chapter 19

GUNS AND SPIES

The next day, my name was called out from the day's roster for firing practice. I held my rifle excitedly. It may not have been the first time I was holding a gun, but this time, I was going to learn to shoot. The weapons instructor, Major Salim, explained the different parts of the gun and showed us how to hold it, aim and shoot. Then another instructor Havildar Baldev Singh took over. 'The real skill with a rifle is not how to shoot it but how to clean it. *Weapon ki safai ki jaankari hai zaroori*. A well-maintained weapon is a reliable weapon,' said Ustad Baldev.

'Arre! Safai again! Why am I always cleaning?' I blurted out before I could stop myself.

I had been loud enough for the ustad to hear me. 'Indira!' he screamed. 'Ten laps around the parade ground with your weapon and pitthu bag.'

There I was again, running around the ground with a rucksack full of sand, this time holding a gun above my head. It was like a rerun of my second day. Only this time, after two laps I was asked to stop running. We'd lost a lot of our weapons in the bombing. We managed to get a few new ones, including Canadian Ross rifles and 303 Lee-Enfields, which had been taken from retreating British forces by the Japanese. Ammunition was precious, so we had to do with the limited dummy rounds we received for practice.

I ran back to the group holding the 303 Lee-Enfield and excitedly asked, 'Can I fire now?'

'Let's learn to use the bayonet first,' Ustad said.

Just up ahead were two figures made of hay, just like scarecrows. 'One is Britain, and the other is America,' Ustad said. 'You will practice on these dummies.'

'Why these names?' asked Harpreet.

'Obviously, one is occupying India, and the other is sending its planes to strike us,' Emily replied.

'March forward. Then strike, pull out and look out. *Maaro, kheencho, dekho,*' commanded Ustad.

'*Maaro, kheencho, dekho! Maaro, kheencho, dekho!*' we yelled as we practised on the hay scarecrows. We stabbed the dummies with the bayonets on our rifles, pulled them out and pretended to look around for the next target.

The next step was sword fighting. The *clank, clank* of the swords excited me, but actually making the sound wasn't easy. 'The sword should feel like an extension of your arm,' said Ustad. He taught us how to stand, how to move our feet while holding the sword and how to treat the sword like it was a part of our bodies. Only after that was I able to go *clank, clank* with the sword.

Finally, we practised firing at the range. I took my position on the ground, resting my rifle on my left hand and the butt of the gun against my shoulder, close to my neck. I then loaded the weapon with a single cartridge and fired a shot.

'Bullseye?' I asked excitedly.

'It hasn't even hit the target,' Ustad replied.

'Where has it gone then?' I asked.

'Choomantar. Vanished.'

'Hey! I fired once but there are two bullet holes on my target. One hit the bullseye and the other is close,' yelled Emily.

'Seems like Indira hit your target, Rosamma. Though we can't say which of you hit the bullseye and which of you missed,' Ustad said.

'It has to be Indira who missed. She's completely missed her target and hit somebody else's,' said Harpreet. Everyone fell about laughing.

Honestly, Emily Rosamma and Harpreet were way better shooters than I was at the time. But I was determined to get better. For that, I had to calm down, focus, really listen to the instructions, watch the more experienced shooters and tell myself that I was there to learn. A few days later, I hit my first bullseye.

'Bravo, Rani Indira! Shabhash! Despite your age and size, you're a good marksman,' Ustad said.

'It's not a person's age or size that matters. It's their skill that matters most. And the Rani regiment has proven that gender doesn't matter either,' said Colonel Malik. He had been watching us from a distance.

Ustad Baldev saluted him. 'Jai Hind, Saheb!' We Ranis saluted him too. 'Jai Hind,' we said. Though the male INA soldiers saluted officers with a 'Saheb', continuing the tradition of the British Indian Army, Netaji had told the Ranis not to do that. It would be just 'Jai Hind' for us.

The colonel summoned me to his office on the firing range. It was a tent with a table and couple a of chairs, which served as the office at the range. Our weapons instructor, Major Swami was sitting across the room while Colonel Malik sat at the table.

'Any more leads on the mole?' he asked.

'I have a few more suspects,' I replied.

'Carry on.'

'Emily.'

'I'm impressed. You're not shying away from suspecting your closest friend.'

'She started training to fire along with me, but she hit the bullseye on her first shot. She seems to have done this before.'

'Excellent. Yes, she's a trained shooter, and a good one at that. She has been training much before you came,' Colonel Malik said. 'She's an agent, but she works for me, not the British.'

'Emily, too?' I asked surprised. 'How did I never pick it up? How come she never told me?' I added.

Colonel Malik simply smiled, 'Neither did you tell her.'

'Emily? Really?' I mumbled.

'Let's just say you are not the only one I assigned tasks to. Now, lets back to the issue at hand.'

'So Emily is ruled out,' I said.

'Here's a lesson for you. You cannot completely rule anyone out, even if they work as an intelligence agent for me. They could be double agents. They could spy for both the INA and the British. You should be cautious and examine possible angles.'

I was shocked. 'Do people do that?'

He laughed. 'You have a lot to learn. Anyway, I have cross checked and have ruled out both Emily and you from suspicion.'

'You suspected me too?' I asked shocked.

'Why not? I just told you to never rule out anyone completely. Now tell me, who's your next suspect?' he asked.

'It could be one of the INA guards at the gate of the Rani camp. They know the location well, and they also interact with people outside the camp.'

'Good. All the people you've mentioned could easily be suspected. We are looking for someone who is totally unseen yet sees everything. Is there anyone else you have in mind?'

'My third suspect is the Burmese girl Sanda, the one who brings hay for the horses.'

'Why do you suspect her?'

'Because she is young like me, does menial work and we often ignore people doing odd jobs. This may have helped her go unnoticed and yet have access to the camp, which no outsider has. She comes in and goes out anytime she pleases, unlike the Ranis, whose movements are restricted. She lives in a village bordering the town with her family. She could be in contact with British sympathisers. Nobody would suspect her. People see right through her, but she sees everything.'

He thought for a minute and asked, 'Presuming, she has passed on inputs to the British, why do you think she might have done it? Could she have any grouse against the INA or against Indian independence?'

'I don't think she's against the INA or Indian independence. She's probably against Japanese rule. I've lived in Burma all my life. I speak their language and have been friends with them. They haven't been treated well by the Japanese. Many girls have been taken prisoners. However, the Japanese have been lenient towards Indians and also towards the Burmese who support the INA. They look at INA sympathisers as Japanese supporters. Sanda's family may have not been troubled by the Japanese. But she may not want to live in fear for long. When the INA marches into India, the Japanese may no longer continue to be lenient towards the Burmese INA sympathisers. Perhaps that's why she may have joined hands with the British,' I reasoned.

'Indira, one part of intelligence is gathering information and the other part is the analysis of that information. The correct analysis of information helps us deduce and predict the enemy's moves and also helps us plan our own moves. You have analysed the information pretty well, at least in this case.' Colonel Malik clapped.

'So, was Sanda a British informant?' I asked.

'As of now, she is a strong suspect. We are still investigating it,' he replied.

'If proven to be a British agent, would you consider her a good agent?' I asked.

'She was an excellent agent. Never attracted any attention, let alone suspicion. A good spy is one who never gets caught,' he replied.

'So, she hasn't been caught yet?' I asked.

'No. Her family has been untraceable after the air raid. That's when we began suspecting her.'

'She must have passed on information in return for safe passage for her family. Can't entirely blame her, if she has really done it,' I said.

'Yes. Soldiers fight for their beliefs, whatever those beliefs may be.'

'And believe that the ones on the opposite side are wrong.' Major Swami, who was quietly listening to us, seated on the other side of the office, spoke for the first time.

'I think it's human nature. Humans do not kill or harm other humans for no reason. We need to believe that our fight is just,' Colonel Malik said.

'Soldiers don't merely follow orders. Soldiering is not just a job. Soldiers need to believe that they are fighting for a higher cause, for the greater good. Only a belief like that can motivate soldiers to lay down their lives,' Major Swami said.

'There can be no greater cause than freedom from slavery for our motherland and our brethren,' said Colonel Malik, and Major Swami nodded in agreement.

Colonel Malik must have noticed me fidgeting, wondering if I should leave, because he said, 'Is there anything else you want to know, Rani Indira?'

'Did you find Madam?' I asked.

'Madam has vanished. She hasn't been seen after the day she was spotted at our gate.'

'So that's all? Nothing could be found about her?' I asked.

'You need to ask the right questions to get the right answers,' Major Swami said, looking down at some papers.

'Yes. Another lesson, Indira. Ask the right questions,' added Colonel Malik.

I thought for a while, before asking, 'What was she selling outside the gate?'

'Wild berries,' came the reply from Colonel Malik.

So that wasn't the right question, I thought. I tried again. 'What was on the papers that the duty officer asked to be burnt?'

'Now you're thinking,' cheered Major Swami.

'Those papers were propaganda leaflets that the British wanted to get to the INA soldiers. The leaflets said that they would be welcomed back if they wanted to return to the British Army. The British have been trying to break the INA, and this was one of their methods,' Colonel Malik said.

'So, Madam works for the British?' I asked.

Colonel Malik nodded. 'She seems to be working with the Allied Forces against the Japanese. You said she gave you fake currency too. The Americans have been pushing in fake currency in all colonies occupied by Japan.'

'Why was she always around when a bombing took place?' I asked.

'She was likely sharing information on possible bombing targets and collecting details on the bombings' effects and the damage to targeted assets,' he said.

'So, she *was* a spy,' I said.

'The signs seem to point in that direction,' Major Swami answered.

'She's partly responsible for my Ma–Baba's killing. Then why did she help my brother and me?' I said, blinking back my tears.

'It's possible she felt guilty' Colonel Malik said.

Major Swami added, 'She must have passed on information about the railway tracks and may not have realised that the people living close to the tracks would get affected too. Most often, ground agents like her are told only to collect inputs. What the higher officers do with the inputs is not known to them.'

'These are just possibilities. Maybe in you and your brother she found two extra pairs of hands to work for her.

Maybe she's genuinely a good-hearted woman and cared for you both,' Colonel Malik said.

'Maybe she's a patriot and is loyal to her land, Burma, and did what she felt she had to to,' Major Swami said.

'She always repeated that Burma should be free of foreign rule. And her dislike of the Japanese was obvious,' I said.

'But we cannot let emotions get in our way. A good soldier is practical and focussed on their target. No distractions allowed,' Major Swami reminded me. He must have sensed the heaviness in my heart when I spoke about Ma–Baba. 'In life, always march forward. There's no looking back. Always think of what lies ahead.'

I lifted my chin and straightened my shoulders. I was no longer a little girl, I reminded myself. I was a soldier.

Someone at the entrance cleared her throat, and saluted, 'Jai Hind.' It was Emily. The colonel must have called her too.

'Jai Hind, Rani Rosamma. Come in. I want you both to join the Bahadur Group. Tomorrow on, you will have special classes along with the other agents,' said Colonel Malik.

Emily and I looked at each other with a twinkle in our eyes. 'Really? Are we going to be spies?'

Colonel Malik simply smiled and dismissed us.

We were going to be spies! We were Netaji's spies. And I would be his youngest spy. Emily and I hugged and jumped up and down in celebration. I would be the best spy—better than Madam.

Chapter 20

EYES AND EARS

I was unable to sleep the whole night. It wasn't because I was nervous—I was just that excited. I smiled so much that my cheeks began hurting. Have you ever felt that? You smile so much that your cheek muscles begin to hurt and you want to smile more but you physically can't. I hadn't been that happy in a very long time. How I wished I could tell Nakul. I imagined his mouth open, his eyes wide. 'What? Really? Is that even possible?' he would say.

I had to share my excitement with somebody. I nudged Emily. 'Isn't it exciting?'

She turned around. She too had been wide awake. 'Yes! We'll be able to go out of the camp and work for India. We don't have to wait to go on the front.'

'What do you mean?'

'I heard the SSG will be the first to go across enemy lines. Way before the others,' she said.

'Will we be part of the SSG?'

'We already are. SSG stands for Special Services Group. It's another name for the Bahadur Group.'

'Oh! The Bahadur Group.'

'Some girls have already been training for quite a while. I heard they signed their names in blood to pledge their loyalty to Netaji.'

'Really?' I wrinkled my nose. 'I don't want to do that. I can't imagine cutting my finger and using that blood as ink,' I said.

'Not much blood. One needle prick and one tiny drop should do. If you're scared of one drop, how will you give up your life for India?' she asked.

'I'll give up my life on the field without batting an eye. Just this ritual seems unnecessary. The thought of hurting myself without reason makes me uneasy.'

'I hope you know if you get caught, you could go to jail and may be tortured,' Emily said.

'I'll never get caught. I'll never go to jail. I'll be like water. The way water evaporates when it is boiled too much, I'll simply vanish into thin air. Choomantar ... whoosh!'

'The most popular and respected freedom fighters in India have all gone to jail. It's brave of them,' Emily said.

'But I'm not just a freedom fighter. I'm a soldier and a spy too. Bravery is not getting caught and going to jail. Bravery is escaping without a trail.'

'Spoken like a true spy-soldier, Rani Indira,' commented Rani Jayashree, who had been pretending to sleep after blowing off the kerosene lamp, but was listening to our conversation.

'Are you awake? We thought you were asleep,' I blurted out.

'A true spy should also be aware of her surroundings. She must be able to collect information but also protect what she knows. Now, it's time for you talkative spies to sleep.' We pulled the blanket over our heads and called it a night.

I must have slept for a couple of hours, when I was shaken awake. 'Wake up, Indira,' said Rani Jayashree. Emily was already sitting up, rubbing her eyes.

'Is it morning already?' she asked.

'No. Two more hours for sunrise,' Rani Jayashree replied.

'Are we getting bombed again?' I asked.

'We don't know. You need to be on watch to alert us. You're both on guard duty tonight at the main gate,' she said.

There was no point arguing about why we were not informed earlier. Well, the duty roster is always made in advance and the Ranis informed of their sentry duty well ahead of time. If we were being informed at the last minute, it was because it was meant to be a punishment. Rani Jayashree wanted us to learn a lesson for keeping awake past bedtime.

Anyway, after the change of guard, we were told the new password and stood with our rifles at the gate. Nobody apart from the Ranis was allowed inside. For anyone else who wanted access, they needed the password, which changed every day.

I tried to memorise that night's password. 'Nobody is going to come at night,' Emily said.

She was right. Nobody came until the wee hours of the morning. At around 5 a.m., we heard the creaking sound of the INA camp gate that was close to our Rani camp. Netaji walked out of the gate and came up to us. 'Jai Hind, Netaji!' Emily and I said to him. He replied and congratulated us. 'I'm proud of you, Indira and Rosamma. You are part of my special group. A whole lot rides on you,' he said.

'Thank you, Netaji. We'll try our best,' Emily said, standing at attention.

I was so happy that Netaji knew about our induction into the Bahadur Group. He kept a track of every Rani and knew each one's progress. Perhaps it was the general excitement or the work of my sleep-deprived mind, but instead of thanking him for the compliment, I asked, 'What do you mean rides on us? Isn't that the work of the fighting soldiers?'

'Yes, it is. But without intelligence, without knowledge of the enemy, without any information, it's like shooting in the dark. You'll miss your target. Spies are the eyes of the army. You'll go across enemy lines even before the infantry. Based on the intelligence you provide, the rest of the army will plan its move. Based on the knowledge a few of you provide, thousands will decide to cross mountains and walk miles,' Netaji said. He began to enter through the gate, when I stopped him.

'Password, please, Netaji,' I said.

'Password? Sorry, I don't know today's password,' he said.

'I cannot let you enter then.'

Emily looked horrified. 'It's Netaji,' she hissed.

'How can I be sure if he's Netaji? There's no proof.'

'But he just spoke to us,' she reasoned. 'It's obviously him!'

'First rule, do not trust anyone,' I replied.

Netaji smiled. 'Are you sure it's not me, Subhas Chandra Bose?'

'You need the password. Rules are rules. No man can enter the Rani camp without knowing the password,' I said.

'All right, let me guess the password,' he said, 'Is it eagle flies?'

I shook my head.

'Eagle soars? The tiger springs? Is it Inquilab Zindabad? No? Okay, I give up!'

'I'm sorry, you cannot enter the camp,' I said. Netaji smiled, nodded and turned to go back to the INA camp.

'What have you done? How could you deny entry to Netaji? We're going to get punished!' cried Emily.

'I did my duty. I followed the rules. That's it,' I said.

When Emily was nervous, she would repeat the same things over and over again. 'That was very wrong, Indira. What you did wasn't right. How could you send Netaji away? He formed the Rani regiment. Why would he need a password?' I began getting worried. What if I was dismissed and sent away from the camp? Where would I go? What about Nakul? I had done what I thought was right, but now I was growing doubtful.

Later that morning, we went to our first training session for the Bahadur Group. I wondered if I would be sent away immediately. We entered the classroom and looked around to see if there were any of our other friends. Many of the Ranis were the educated girls. We all greeted each other with 'Jai Hind', yet I caught some of them whispering behind my back. 'She's the girl who sent Netaji away.' So, the news had spread. Such incidents cannot be hidden. They have a way of getting out. Perhaps Netaji might have told it to someone and joked about it, or could be the INA guards who were watching from their gate. I don't know how, but everyone knew about it.

Major Swami, who set up the intelligence school, was waiting for us. After I introduced myself, he called out, 'Indira ... the girl who turned Netaji away.' I was stunned.

'Nobody has done this to him before,' he continued. 'The commander of the INA was refused entry into the camp of the army he raised!' He laughed loudly, and the other Ranis joined in. Emily giggled too!

I felt like a fool. I blurted out, 'The instructions were to allow entry only when the password is said. Nobody mentioned there were exceptions.'

'There are no exceptions,' Major Swami said. The laughter died down. 'Netaji is impressed with your sincerity and has been praising you.'

Roopa Ganguly, one of the Ranis who was training to be an officer, said, 'Shouldn't she have applied some common sense? It was Netaji, after all. Everyone recognises him.'

'Well, Netaji was once placed under house arrest in Calcutta. The British police thought they would recognise him if he ever tried to escape. Netaji grew a beard and dressed as a Pathan named Mohammed Ziauddin and escaped to Peshawar,' Major Swami said.

Netaji, we learnt, was a master of disguise. On entering Afghanistan, he disguised himself as a local Afghan tribesman. He didn't know Pashto and knew this could blow his cover. So he pretended to be deaf and mute. He changed his appearance again and travelled to Moscow on an Italian passport. Pretending to be an Italian, he travelled to Rome and then to Germany. When he had to secretly travel out of Germany, he did so in a submarine and reached Singapore.

'Netaji himself set up intelligence schools, the Azad Schools, in various camps. He's keen that you are all trained well, for some among you will be the first to go across enemy lines,' Major Swami said.

'Wow!' Emily said, elbowing me.

I made up my mind then: I too would be a master of disguise, just like Netaji.

'We're going to outdo Japanese intelligence. The Japanese spies helped in the fall of Singapore and helped in the attack on Pearl Harbour in America. In the same way, we will bring victory to the INA and free India,' said Roopa.

'Yes, the Fall of Singapore is the British Army's greatest defeat,' Major Swami said. I was all ready for him to start with the practical lessons, but he began with telling us some history. You know that feeling when you're excited to do something fun in class but then the teacher starts telling you a story that never seems to end? That's exactly what happened when Major Swami went on talking to us about the Battle of Singapore.

The story went like this. The British were really proud of their colony, Singapore. They called it the Gibraltar of the East, because they believed it was unconquerable. They figured Singapore could be attacked only through the sea by a navy. So, they put all their focus on sea defences. Meanwhile, the Japanese had their spies posted as fisherfolk and port workers to learn all about the British plans. The only other way into Singapore was through a thin strip of land connecting Thailand to Malaya. It was covered in thick forests, and everyone thought this strip was too difficult to march through. The British figured they'd see soldiers marching in from so many kilometres away because of how hard that stretch was to cross, so they didn't focus much on this area. But then the Japanese surprised the British forces by cycling through the forests and attacking them. It was the first time an attack was led on cycles.

In the Battle of Singapore, the Japanese and the British were equally battered. Both sides were running low on everything: soldiers, food, fuel and ammunition. But the Japanese were good at gathering intelligence and equally good at guarding their information. They acted like they were in a better position than the British and were ready to go to battle, even though they weren't ready at all at that time. The British thought there was no way they could win with a counterstrike when they had so little left. So they surrendered. The British accepted defeat before trying, only because they didn't have all the information. If the British had pushed back after a Japanese attack, who knows? They might have retained Singapore, and history would have been totally different.

'Maybe the INA would never have been raised. The Rani regiment would not have taken shape. We wouldn't have been here,' said Roopa, the know-it-all.

'Maybe not,' Major Swami replied.

When the Japanese took over, they gave the Indian soldiers in the British Army a choice: become prisoners of war or form the Free Army to fight for India's freedom from the British. Captain Mohan Singh gathered many soldiers and formed the Azad Fauj.

'When Netaji took over the reins of the INA, patriotism soared. More soldiers joined. Even civilians enlisted in the Free Army. People donated money and even sold their jewellery to help him strengthen the army that would liberate India,' added know-it-all Roopa.

'Right. The reason I've told you this background is so that you realise that whatever you'll be doing in the future is crucial. It's not like running errands. You are the eyes and ears of the army. Without intelligence, it's like shooting aimlessly in the dark,' he said.

How far I'd come from housekeeping and cooking at the camp. I was the eyes and ears of the army!

'The Japanese attack on Pearl Harbour was a huge shock to the Americans, who thought they were invincible. That attack too involved months of spying and planning. Japanese agents worked at the ports as fisherfolk and tourists to gather information. Planning, strategy, tactics—nothing can take place without reliable intelligence. A battle is fought on the ground, but before that, it is fought in the mind,' said the major.

I was fighting to stay awake by the end of these stories. But I had to give Major Swami one thing—he made me feel like what I was about to learn was really important. I guess it's only when you believe that whatever you are learning is vital that you are able to learn well. If you don't believe in it, you can't study a subject properly.

'So, due credit should be given to the Japanese secret service agents for their victory at Singapore, Pearl Harbour and for the formation of the INA, right?' asked you-know-who.

'Absolutely. I hope all of you will help the Azad Hind Fauj defeat the British,' said Major Swami.

In the coming weeks, we learnt map reading. We had to learn the symbols associated with different topographical features and landmarks. There is a symbol for a cross road, a pagoda or a temple, a symbol for river, bridge and so on.

'The most important are the symbols to denote enemy positions,' our instructor said and asked us to memorise the symbols for posts, platoons, battalions, brigades, division, ammunition dumps and so on. 'These give the information of enemy strength at particular locations. We can deduce the number of soldiers and their assets at a particular location,' he added.

'I can only see dots, lines—horizontal lines, vertical lines, thick lines and thin lines, slanting lines, arrows and circles, Indira. One standing line is this, two standing line is that and slanting line is something else. Ayyo!' Emily complained.

'I now understand how helpful alphabets are,' I replied. Emily scribbled her name in Tamil, and again scribbled something else that looked different. 'This is Laxmi in Tamil,' she said. I imitated her hand movements and scribbled the same.

'Focus on learning MR- map reading,' he chided us.

The educated Ranis fared better than us in map reading and found Morse code easy. When it came to disguises, covert operations and sabotaging enemy assets, we estate girls fared better than them.

All of us waited for our assignment. The educated Ranis were expected to get their assignments first. Then, the unexpected happened. Colonel Malik summoned me to his office one day. 'Do you speak Burmese?' he asked.

'Yes. I speak other languages too,' I replied.

'What about Nepali?'

'Yes, I speak that too. I learnt it from some of the Nepali railway employees,' I said.

'Great. You'll enter India as a Burmese worker. With your knowledge of Nepali, you'll earn the trust of the Gurkha soldiers in the British Indian Army and get intel from them,' he said. 'What other languages do you speak?'

'Hindi, Oriya, English, Bangla. Emily has taught me a little Tamil too.'

'Fantastic. Emily Rosamma will join you. There are battalions with Tamil-speaking soldiers too. You'll both leave tomorrow before sunrise.'

'But I still have a lot more to learn, Will I be able to pull off an operation?' I doubted.

'Not everything can be taught in a classroom. Theoretical knowledge and practically being on field amidst the enemy are two different things. With your experience of surviving on your own, I believe you will do just fine. Being a child, you will not easily attract suspicion,' he said.

Just like that, I was ordered to enter India, crossing enemy lines as a spy.

I was going home.

Before that, I had to meet Nakul. I didn't know when I would see him again. My future was unpredictable and my mission difficult. 'Nakku, I'm going for a special training. I may not be able to meet you for a few days,' I said.

'What special training? Where are you going?' he asked.

'Somewhere ahead of Maymyo,' I lied. Everyone knew that a contingent was moving to Maymyo, and we were to leave the camp at the same time along with the contingent and separate at a diversion enroute.

'I heard some officers say a hospital is being set up in Maymyo. Are you going to train as a nurse there?' he asked.

'I guess so,' I replied. I so badly wanted to tell him the truth. Share my excitement. Make plans for our future. Create stories from my adventures to tell him. He would have loved that. But a good spy never reveals her plans, not even to her most loved ones.

'Nursing is good. Maybe the training will make you kinder,' he said with a smile. 'I heard from the nurses who come here that their training here will help them land jobs when the war is over.'

'That's true. Rani Kalpana's parents agreed to her joining the INA only after she convinced them she will get trained as a nurse and find work in a hospital after the war,' I said.

'That sounds good! We could work in a hospital together,' he said excitedly.

I hugged him one last time. 'Be good. Eat well. Stay away from trouble. Take good care of yourself,' I said.

'You sound like Ma,' he said.

At dawn, Emily and I left for our mission.

Chapter 21

SNAKES AND RIVERS

'Have you ever wondered if trees are really dancing girls who somehow turned into wood and are still holding their dancing poses?' Emily asked, looking up at the jungle. I wasn't as awestruck as her since I'd grown up playing in the jungles of Burma.

'What do you mean?' I asked.

'Look at this tall tree. It's almost touching the sky. And this creeper around it has grown so thick that it's like a twisting tree itself. The two together look like a dancing girl and her swaying saree,' she said.

'Huh, I never looked at them like that. These strong climbers are like stairs to me. They make it easier to climb straight trees.'

'Look at this one. How beautiful!' She walked up to a tree. I was least interested in admiring the trees—I couldn't stop thinking about the assignment. I had my eyes fixed on the ground to avoid tripping over anything. 'Look at the patches on this fat climber. What beautiful patterns!' Before I could say 'Don't!', Emily had touched it.

'It's so cold!' she said.

'Emily, that's a Burmese python!' I screamed.

'Chhee!' she screamed and took to her heels. I followed her.

'Stop!' I shouted when I caught up to her.

'No, don't stop!' she yelled over her shoulder. 'The python! We're running away from the python!'

'I don't think the python is following us. I don't think it even cares that you touched it. It must have just wrapped itself around a tree after eating to crush the bones of its lunch,' I replied.

'Won't it swallow us?' she asked, panting.

'I don't think so. We're too big for it.'

'I might be too big for it, but not you, Indira. You're puny.'

'I guess it could gobble me up like it gobbles up a dog or a deer,' I said.

'Let me share a tip I learnt while working on the plantations. If a python gets holds of you and starts swallowing you, stand still holding your sickle straight. As the python keeps going up thinking it's eating you, it will go on cutting itself against your sickle and will eventually get split into two halves,' she said.

'You mean like splitting a bamboo? You hit the bamboo with a sickle and then you can run it down and split the stick into two, isn't it?' I said.

'Yes. Easy as splitting green bamboo. A dry brown bamboo takes too much effort.'

'Why would the python keep moving ahead if it keeps getting hurt? Won't it feel the pain?' I asked.

'I don't know. This is an old wives' tale. Sometimes, it's good to just believe them without questioning them too much. Anyway, a sickle can definitely help in case of any attack,' she replied.

We'd managed to get some distance away from the snake, but we were still deep in the jungle. We had to navigate through it and cross into India. The journey from the Rani camp had been long and tiring. First, we were taken to an INA base, which was close to the border. The INA and the Japanese Imperial Army were setting up their base there to get ready to attack the British Indian forces and march into India. Before that, we had to enter enemy camps and get whatever information we could. Disguised as local Burmese girls, Emily and I took a cart ride up to the edge of the jungle and then had to walk through it so as not to look suspicious. Just as we were Netaji's secret agents, there could be British Army agents too in the area who could blow our cover. They were spread all over the border villages and along the roads. We had to avoid their eyes. So, we had to trek some distance. Luckily, all those long marches—in full gear and carrying weapons and rations—we'd done during our training came in handy. At least this time, we had no heavy weapons or bags filled with sand, just what we needed.

'Do you think we're going in the right direction?' asked Emily.

'I'm not sure. We could have gone off track when we ran away from the python.'

'Check your compass.'

'North is that way.' I pointed to my right.

'Okay, then we keep walking straight.'

But when you have to dodge thickets and walk zigzag through the maze of trees, you can't really follow a straight road.

'What is this huge heap of crushed cardboard?' asked Emily.

'Elephant dung.'

'Oh! I thought for a second it was something left by the enemy,' she said.

'There must be some elephants migrating along these routes,' I guessed.

'I heard they migrate through the same road every migration season. Apparently, the route doesn't change for over a thousand years,' Emily said.

'Really? How do they remember? Maybe they tell their children,' I said. 'Perhaps the mother elephant teaches the kids while the father elephant leads the way.'

'No, no! Interesting fact: elephant herds are led by the mother,' Emily said.

I laughed. 'You mean elephants also have Rani regiments.'

'Seems so. I heard even among lions, it's the female, the lioness, who hunts. The male doesn't!'

'Then among humans, why do they say that women shouldn't go out to work, let alone go to war? Thank God Netaji and the Rani of Jhansi Regiment will change this,' I said.

'Do you remember Netaji's speech the other day? He said that when the Rani Regiment marches into India and fights with valour, the British Indian soldiers will feel ashamed. They will drop their weapons and come join the INA. With no Indian soldiers, the British Empire will fall and they'll flee from India.'

'I heard him and the other officers also address us as Amazons. Do you know what that means?' I asked.

'In some ancient mythology, Amazons were female warriors. They led and won many battles. They were braver and more skilled in warfare than the men,' she replied.

'Are they still around?'

'I don't think so. They now call Amazons a myth. People doubt they ever existed. Men might have felt insecure about these brave, strong women and erased them from history,' she answered.

'People now make young girls believe that they're weak and can never become warriors. Even my brother and I were shocked to see women soldiers.'

'And we're going to take advantage of this assumption. Nobody is going to suspect us. You're going to be the weak young child and I your older sister,' said Emily.

We had been walking for some time now, but the stream we'd marked earlier that day on our map was nowhere to be seen.

'How many elephants do you think are in this jungle? Or is it just one elephant?' Emily asked.

'I'm not sure. Why do you ask?'

'Is this the same elephant dung we crossed some time ago?' she asked.

I looked at it for a minute. 'I can't tell.'

'Do you remember the shape? Was it like this? A dry-mud-mound-like thing?' Emily said.

'Hmm ... you said it was like crushed cardboard,' I said.

'Well, this also looks like crushed cardboard,' she said.

'All elephant dung looks like that. How do we know if it's the same mound?'

Emily pulled out the map from the bag slung over her shoulder. 'As per this, we should have reached the Chindwin River by now.'

'While we were talking of matriarch elephants, I was looking at this heap of leaves at the base of this bamboo tree and wondering about king cobras. I think we've already crossed this bamboo grove. We've been going in circles,' I said.

'Silly us. We've lost so much time. No more chit-chatting now,' said Emily.

'Okay, okay. Here, I'm stitching my lips with a needle and thread.' I pretended to sew my lips shut and we changed our direction.

'So, what were you wondering about king cobras?' Emily asked.

'They're the only snakes who build nests with dry leaves. I was wondering if that heap of dry leaves was a king cobra nest.'

'It's getting dark, and we need to be very careful. It's not only British agents and Burmese rebels who are dangerous—it's also wild creatures in the jungle. Danger around and on the ground,' Emily warned.

'And above.' I pointed to an airplane flying high above us. We hid under a big tree. The airplane circled around and then flew off. It seemed like it dropped some light things. 'What did they drop? Some dry leaves or feathers?' I asked.

'I can't tell, but whatever they are, they're very light. They're flying away in the breeze,' Emily said.

'Here, here.' I jumped and caught one. It was a paper pamphlet printed with an illustration of an Indian soldier sitting around a fire with his wife and children in his village. The text was in Hindustani, written in the English alphabet on one side and in Urdu on the other side. It read, 'It's been long since you met your family. Don't you want to return to your homes? We understand that you had to join the Japanese to survive, but it's time to come back to us. No punishment awaits you. We will give you safe passage back to the arms of your loved ones. The Japanese are using you to fight their war. When they're defeated, you'll lose your chance to return to your families. Return to the British Indian Army and we will welcome you.'

'What is this?'

'Propaganda leaflet,' Emily replied. 'They are urging the INA soldiers to put down their arms and return to the British Army. They want to dismantle Netaji's army.'

'Well, we won't let that happen,' I said through gritted teeth as we marched on.

Finally, we came to the river in the map. The land across the river was under British occupation. The river, along with the hills on either side, acted like a natural fence between the two territories. It was mainly the river that kept the Japanese forces from entering British India and kept the British forces from coming back to Burma.

We chose to stay behind a huge rock on a hilltop. We watched the people on the other side of the river. The height helped us get a better view. Emily and I took turns to watch and note things down. I preferred climbing the tall teak tree and watching from there. Night fell and I was careful not to fall from the tree.

The next morning, we headed to the narrowest part of the river. 'Do you think we can swim across?' I asked.

'I doubt it. The current could carry us away. And I'm not sure how deep it can get,' Emily replied.

'Then let's build a raft,' I suggested.

We cut down bamboos and made grooves with our pocketknives, and then tied them together to create a raft.

It took us an entire day. We saved the longest bamboo stick to row with. We crawled onto the raft. 'Careful. Don't put all your weight on it at once. The raft may tilt,' Emily said.

Emily held one end of the raft to keep it steady until I got on. She pushed it farther into the river until the water rose to her neck. 'Now it's your turn to keep the raft steady, Indira,' she said as she carefully climbed on. We sat on opposite ends to balance the weight. Emily then stood up and pushed the long bamboo stick into the riverbed and pushed the raft ahead. By the time we made it to the shore, she was exhausted.

'Let me hide the boat,' she said as soon as we were on the bank.

'No, let's dismantle it and not leave a trace,' I said.

'What if we need it when we return?' she argued.

'What if British soldiers or their spies spot this and get suspicious? We can't risk it,' I said.

Emily nodded. 'You're right. We can't let anything sabotage our mission.' We opened the knots and threw the bamboo sticks into the river.

'This is like burning bridges and leaving no route to retreat,' Emily said.

'Ah, that reminds me. I should make a note of this,' I said.

Chindwin River narrows towards the south. No bridge in sight. Depth ranges from 4 feet to 10 feet. Vegetation is mostly teak and bamboo. Area around banks is hilly and steep. No patrols spotted.

'Do you think this information is helpful?' I asked, showing Emily the notes.

'Yes, of course. Terrain inputs are very important. It helps the army decide its course of action,' she replied.

'How?'

'If our army knows there is no bridge, they will find alternate routes of attack. If they believe the depth and width of the river is not dangerous, some infantry teams could swim across. And knowing about the hills and plains will help the Japanese Army and the Azad Hind Fauj decide if tanks and artillery guns can be used,' she explained.

The first enemy camp was a few kilometres cross the river. Tired of the long trek, I wished that the camp close by was our destination, but it was not to be.

'I wish I could just hang my legs up and drain out the tiredness, just like we hang washed clothes on a clothesline and let the water drip down,' I said.

'And I wish someone would massage my legs with coconut oil,' Emily said.

'Why don't we look for a ride?' I suggested.

'We could. We have been trekking to infiltrate without having to go through check posts and to avoid suspicion while crossing across. Since we have already infiltrated inside British occupied territory, we could try to find some means of transport,' she said.

'Now we have to find the road,' I said. Just then Emily, her eyes wide, placed her forefinger on her lips and gestured for me to be silent. We could hear the faint beating of drums. 'Perhaps there's a village close by,' I whispered.

'Yes. There could be. In that direction,' Emily pointed, and we walked towards the sound.

We reached a busy village. It was market day, so traders and shoppers crowded the streets. I found a good lookout in a tree just outside the village, while Emily blended into the crowd, making mental notes of everything she saw and heard.

At dusk, a cloth merchant loaded a bullock cart and strapped a tarpaulin over the cart, ready to move to another market the next day. When the village fell silent and everyone seemed to have gone to sleep, Emily and I carefully slipped under the tarpaulin and into the cart. The bundles of cloth made for a soft, cozy bed. Though we both desperately wanted to sleep, we had to be cautious. We took turns sleeping to keep a lookout at all times. At sunrise, the bullock cart started moving, and we did our best to stay quiet and unnoticed. After a couple of hours, a damp, earthy smell told us we were near water. We could smell wet wood too. Peeking out, we saw that we were at a river.

'Have we gone in the opposite direction? Are we back at the Chindwin River?' I whispered.

'I don't know. Let's just get out,' Emily said, and we jumped out of the moving cart.

The river was narrower than the Chindwin, and wooden boats were docked to ferry people across. That explained the smell of damp wood.

'It's the Myittha River. It's on the map,' I said to Emily.

'Oh, thank God! We've come to the right place,' she said, and we got on to a ferry along with other villagers waiting to cross over.

Crossing the river marked the start of another long trek. For four long days, we walked through jungles, climbed up and down hills, and rolled down slopes, ending up with bruises on our arms and sores on our feet. When you're that tired, you don't have the energy to even talk. And even if you do, you don't remember the conversations. The only thing I remember is when Emily said, 'I think we're finally here,' pointing to an old milestone that said, 'Tedim - 5 km.'

Our mission was to sneak into the military station at Tedim, which was the headquarters of the 17th Division of the British Indian Army. It was thought to be impossible to get into.

As we got closer to the military station, we left the road and entered deeper into the forest, climbed a small hill and found shelter under a rock by a huge banyan tree. 'Let's check for snakes and scorpions,' Emily said.

'I'm sure they're around. After all, it's a jungle,' I replied.

'But you don't want to sit on top of one, do you?' Emily said sternly.

We dug a square trench and put up a tent in the middle. First, though, we had to secure our bags with our belongings and ration. We dug a hole in the ground, lined it with a piece of canvas sheet and put our belongings in it. We then covered it with twigs that were longer than the barely one-feet-long mouth of the hole, and placed some leaves over it.

Rebuilding the Rani camp after the Allied Forces bombed us had taught us a lot. Of course, the never-ending training under our strict teachers helped too. But it was maybe our background of working on plantations or, in my case, surviving without parents and hiding in the jungles that helped the most. We might have even been more skilled than the officers. In battle, it's not school certificates but life skills, presence of mind and courage that are most handy.

The next morning, we climbed up on a hilltop that gave us a clear view of the military station.

I kept track of when the guards would switch shifts, since our chance to get in was better around this time. But first, we had to look like we belong there. We casually strolled past collecting firewood and grass. At the end of the day, we carried back our haul. Emily could perfectly balance her pile on her head without having to touch it. She'd learnt how to do this at the plantation. We repeated this for a few days, going at the same time and returning at the same time.

One morning, one of the guards smiled when he saw us.

'We've now blended into our surroundings. We're as good as the grass growing here,' I said.

'Yes, our routine has paid off. When the same things are done again and again, onlookers tend to ignore them. They can see us, acknowledge us, yet do not notice us enough to suspect us,' she said and went on to imitate our instructor's gruff tone, 'You cannot help being seen. You are not ghosts, you see. The trick is to be seen, yet remain unnoticed. That is what is to be invisible.'

First step: Blend in. Be seen, yet become invisible. Mission accomplished!

Chapter 22

A WAY WITH HERBS

Next step: Gain entry into the enemy camp.

Only exchanging smiles wasn't going to do the job. We had to give the soldiers something they'd want. Emily and I went herb hunting in the forest.

'What about these?' I said, pointing to a cluster of weeds.

'Yes, good. They help beat jaundice,' Emily said.

I dug into the soil and pulled out a piece of tree root. 'My mother said this keeps evil spirits away.'

'These berries cure an upset stomach,' said Emily.

'And these herbs can heal wounds.'

'Are you sure?' Emily asked.

'Does it matter? All that matters is that they believe us,' I replied.

With our little collection, we went back to the gates of the military station. I approached the guard who had smiled at us.

'Would you like to buy some desi medicines?' I asked. 'We have jadi-booti for all ailments. We forest dwellers have been using them for ages.'

'We don't need them,' he snubbed and looked at us sternly. 'We have English medicines.'

'English medicines are effective only against English diseases. These Englishmen don't understand our native culture, let alone the illnesses specific to this region,' I replied.

'We have medicines for fever, dysentery, even small pox. What do you mean "illnesses specific to this region"? There's no such thing,' he shot back.

'What about malaria?' I asked.

'What about it?'

'You know that malaria is more prevalent in these jungles than anywhere else. You've travelled, served the crown in different parts of the world. Have you seen huge, sly mosquitoes like these anywhere else?'

'Hmm ... these mosquitoes *are* different. When they bite, the itch stays for a long time,' he said.

'Where are you from?' I asked.

'Nepal.'

'*Timi Nepali ho!*' I switched to Nepali. 'You are a brave Gurkha, brother.'

'Yes, sister,' he said, unable to keep the smile off his face. We spoke about our homes and how I knew Nepali. I told him that a Nepali family had given me shelter after my parents were killed during the Japanese invasion of Burma.

Before he could ask any more questions, I quickly asked, 'Do you have mosquitoes like these in Nepal?'

'Not like these.'

'Here, we have these killer mosquitoes. One bite can be fatal. Can you imagine something so tiny taking the lives of tough warriors like you? But it happens all the time.'

'Yes, I've been told that more soldiers die of malaria than from bullets,' he replied.

'Haven't you wondered how the locals don't get affected as much as all of you do? That's because we have age-old wisdom passed on to us by our ancestors—rituals and herbs that appease the gods.'

'So, what do you have?'

'These herbs will drive away mosquitoes. Use them to create smoke and no mosquito will dare come near you,' I said, handing over dry lemongrass. The things Madam had taught Nakul and me were proving helpful.

'What do I owe you?' he asked.

'Well, just one person paying me won't be helpful. I need more customers. Could you please take my herbs inside and sell them? Then you can give me the money.'

'No, I can't sell anything for you. I'm not doing that,' he said.

'But how will I make any money then? All right, at least let me in,' I replied.

'I'll let only one of you in. Which of you will go in?' he asked.

'I'll go. I'm the older one,' said Emily.

'No, not you. Let the younger one go. She's trustworthy,' he declared and let me in.

The British military station was huge, bustling with soldiers and some local villagers who worked there. I saw some villagers cutting the wild vegetation, some were manicuring the lawns, some watering ornamental plants, some were involved in some construction work. I saw one woman whose gait was like Ma's, hustling and walking briskly as though she was late for work. At that moment, I remembered the old days with Ma. Old memories flashed before my eyes. Ma too walked briskly to go to work at Saheb's house. Perhaps, this woman was also working at a British officer's house.

I manage to sell more lemongrass, but my best-selling product was the root that I had randomly dug out. 'Keep this root under your pillow and no evil spirits will come near you,' I said to the soldiers walking by me.

'You know, the other day, I felt like someone was following me but there was nobody else there,' said one soldier of the British Indian army.

'These jungles are filled with spirits. Don't ever turn around if you feel that same sensation,' I warned.

'No wonder! My friend felt something like that and turned around to see if anyone was there. Later that night, he got a high fever that didn't go away for three days.'

'What did he see? Did he see small knee-high creatures? Two bulging eyes but no other features on their face?' I knew many of the legends the Burmese believed in. Now was my time to use them to my advantage.

'Yes, yes! That's what he saw,' said the soldier.

'There are two kinds of these creatures. Either white or black. If you see the white ones, there's nothing to worry about. But if you spot the black ones, run for your lives,' I said.

His eyebrows shot up. 'What if we don't want to see either of them?' he asked.

'In that case, keep a piece of this root with you at all times. It has magical properties that will ward off all unearthly spirits.'

'How does a young girl like you know all this?' another soldier asked.

'All of us know this, even children younger than me. It's like we're born with this ancestral knowledge. My parents began teaching me how to listen to my inner voice and recognise different herbs and roots when I was just a toddler,' I said. Honestly, I could tell that what I was saying didn't make much sense, but people easily believe you if you sound mysterious.

'The old woman in our village said things like this too,' he said.

Since I had lived and interacted with the INA soldiers, it was easy for me to understand the needs and fears of the British Indian soldiers. After all, the INA soldiers had been a part of the British Army before joining Netaji. My visits became regular, and each day I went with a new story to sell the herbs. In just a few days, I had a broad idea about the layout of the barracks, the guard posts, their shift timings, the location of the watchtowers, the various entrances and exits, the names of the officers, and the specifics of the battalions stationed at Tedim. I noted down everything you could see from the roads within the camp, drawing my own map of it all.

One evening, while Emily and I were about to sleep in on the hilltop, we had a visitor. A beggar, with long, unkempt hair, a scruffy beard, a ripped kurta and a dirty cloth tied around his waist. He carried a sack and collected garbage in it. Nobody would have dared look into his gunny sack. They definitely wouldn't have thought he was a trained soldier. But I instantly recognised him. 'Bishnu Da!' I called out. 'You stink,' I said, pinching my nose.

He laughed. 'This stink keeps away British sympathisers.'

He was part of the Bahadur Group and was our courier. He carried messages and information from us to pass on to our handler. We did not know who our handler was. We only knew that he was an officer who passed orders and collected inputs from us through Bishnu Da.

We told him what we had learnt. The most important thing I had noticed was who made up the troops. I had found out why the Tedim forces were considered unbeatable. This station had an all-Gurkha brigade. The Gurkhas are considered the bravest soldiers, and undefeatable. Most British Army brigades posted in the region had three battalions: a British battalion, an Indian battalion and a Gurkha battalion. This station was unlike the rest. It was all Gurkhas.

'Do you think this information will be useful?' I asked Bishnu Da.

'Definitely. For one, the INA has been hoping that when they attack to enter India, the British Indian troops will lay their weapons down and join us to fight against the British. But that won't happen with Nepali soldiers. The Gurkhas are fiercely loyal to those they serve,' he said.

'Do you think the British know INA's plan?,' Emily asked.

'They could. They have spies too,' he replied.

'Are there INA spies other than us in this location?' I whispered.

'Yes!' he whispered back, smiling. 'The Bahadur Group has made many British Indian soldiers posted in the southern region leave the British Army and join the INA. The agents infiltrated the camps, mingled with the soldiers and told them the progress we have made. We have told them how we will defeat the British with Japanese help and free India. See, we have distributed pamphlets too,' he said pulling out a paper from a bag, which had an illustration of Netaji riding a Tiger and a outline of India's map with broken chains.

'So, we're making progress,' Emily said.

'Yes. The Subhas Brigade and the Gandhi Brigade are getting ready to march into India,' Bishnu Da revealed.

'So, keep your eyes and ears open for any intel. Try to find out if the British know of our plans. Keep note of any new movements towards Fort White in the south.'

He wanted more specific information from us too: maps, attack plans, details about supply lines, the strength of troops and location of armouries, ammunition dumps, the location of air fields, the details of bridges over rivers. The list went on.

To get this intel, we had to get more access. Selling evil spirit repellent wasn't going to do that, and I was beginning to attract too much attention with my herbs. I had to find a way to enter officially every day and lay low. Sneaking in by sweet-talking and bribing the guard wasn't going to work again.

I had to get closer to where the action was: the administrative blocks, the offices, the officers' mess and the officers' residences. But there was no way I could sell the 'evil spirits' story to the officers.

The mission had got more challenging.

Chapter 23

FROG HUNT

While I tried to figure out how to get to the residences of the officers, Emily had started working at a cattle shed in town. She didn't speak the local language very well, so she pretended to be mute and agreed to work for far less than what was due. 'Did you get this idea from Netaji, who pretended to be mute in Afghanistan?' I asked.

'Yes. And anyway, it's always safer to be silent. When we speak too much, we unintentionally give out information. All I need for this job is to listen and watch,' she replied.

While she tended to the cattle and cut grass around the farms and in the forest, she made mental notes. Most of the villagers were sympathetic to the British and didn't want a Japanese invasion. We were worried about this interfering with the INA's efforts to march into India.

'There are still British officers stranded in Burma and in hiding. I recently saw the villagers get one British officer from Burma across to British-controlled land in Manipur,' she said.

'How did they get him away from under the Japanese?' I asked.

'The villagers know these jungles very well. It's not difficult for them to smuggle anything and anyone. They get paid well for this, I'm sure.'

Emily found some tribal leaders in nearby towns who were open to the idea of swarajya, or self-rule. They admired Netaji and wanted to help the INA. She passed their names on to Bishnu Da.

'Good work, Rosamma. We need local support to overthrow the British,' he said.

'Will they help our forces when we march here?' I asked.

'We'll have to grow a bond with them and nurture the relationship. These things don't happen overnight. INA representatives will meet these people in disguise, negotiate and forge an alliance,' Bishnu Da explained. 'What progress have you made?' he asked me.

'I'm working on it,' I replied sheepishly.

'Get help from Rosamma if you need it. Remember, good soldiers always work in teams and help each other. A single soldier cannot win a war.'

'Emily and I have each other's back. We're sisters in arms,' I said.

'I'm looking out for ways to help Indira. Together, we'll win,' Emily said.

'Remember, there's no Azad Hind Fauj without teamwork. There's no march to Delhi. There's no promise of freedom. *Kadam kadam mila ke chal*. March together, work together.' With that, he left.

I didn't like that Bishnu Da had lectured me. And Emily didn't appreciate that he assumed she wasn't helping me. We were good friends. We had undergone gruelling training together, withstood a bombardment, and trekked the jungles together. Emily had also taught me to write my name in Tamil.

She sighed. 'We girls always have to prove ourselves, no matter how progressive men are. Old prejudices always cloud their minds.'

'What did his comments have to do with us being girls?' I asked.

'Men believe that two women can never live together without quarrelling. They think women are always jealous of each other. I think that's what he was hinting at. If we were men, he would have just agreed that our job is difficult,' she said.

The camp was a huge area with lot of open spaces, neatly paved pathways and also parts of forests and wildlife too. It was a village in its own way. Access to common areas were easy. As the days passed, it became clear just how tough it was to gain entry to the offices, mess and residences.

Emily would come back every day and tell me what she'd overheard about the camp at the village. 'You never know what little piece of information could be handy,' she'd say.

One day, Emily came running back from the cattle shed. Two soldiers had come to the shed to order grass to feed the officers' favourite horses. One of the spoilt horses liked to only eat a particular kind of fresh grass from the grasslands, not what grew inside the military station. Emily's boss asked her to collect the grass and deliver it.

'We've found our ticket to get in officially. We're the horse feed girls,' she said.

We carried fresh grass and hay inside the camp and up to the British officer's house, entry around which was restricted for us earlier. The white bungalow with high walls and slanting roof with red tiles stood out against the blue sky. His batman, an Indian soldier who looked after officer's requirements and managed his house, saw us and pointed us towards the direction of the stable, and asked us to drop off the grass there. Incidentally, the officer too was at the stable, caressing his horse.

'Good morning, sir,' I greeted. The British officer didn't even look in my direction. He simply mounted his horse and rode away. I had practised my speech the previous night, but I didn't get a chance to say it. The next day, we were back around the same time, and encountered the officer again. I tried greeting him once again, but I got the same response—nothing. I was hoping to gain his attention and perhaps be granted permission to come every day or perhaps gain some other employment in his house. I persisted. On the third day, I once again greeted him. This time, he simply smirked and rode away.

'Why do you want to talk to him? Saheb doesn't speak to natives without good cause,' said his batman.

'I just wanted to see how gora sahebs speak,' I replied. 'Do they sound different?'

He laughed. 'They do. Their mouths don't open enough to make Indian sounds.'

'Maybe it's because it's so cold in Britain, so they open their mouths as little as possible to speak,' I said.

'You should see him open his mouth to eat frogs. Aah!' He opened his mouth wide.

'Frogs?' I asked.

'Yes, chhe, chhe. He loves eating frog legs. Particularly those of the yellow ones that come out after it rains.'

'Where does he get them?' I asked.

'The villagers get them for him.'

'But I haven't seen anyone bringing them in recently,' I said.

'Do you keep watch over who comes here?' he asked, one eyebrow raised.

'No, no. I mean if somebody carried frogs in, it would definitely attract attention, isn't it?' I replied quickly. 'There would be a *gutur-gutur* sound coming from the bag.'

'Yes, he likes frogs. He checks to see if they're fresh, the way we check fish.'

'I know a place in the jungle which has a clean waterbody that has big, fleshy frogs,' I suggested.

'Okay. Get them. I will decide if they are better than regular frogs,' said the batman handing over an earthen pot.

On our trek through the jungle to find the camp, I had noticed a pond with bright yellow frogs. At first, Emily and I thought they were yellow flowers, water lilies perhaps. When we looked closer, we saw that each flower had two bulging eyes watching us.

When I told Emily we needed to go back to the pond, she pulled a face. 'Oh no! Not that yukky frog kingdom,' she said.

'But we need to catch them for the British officer's meal.'

'Why does he want frogs?' she asked.

'Some people find them delicious and relish them.'

'I suppose every culture has different eating habits,' she said.

'I've been on frog hunts. That experience is going to come in handy now,' I said.

'I've seen people in the nearby villages smoke the frogs and preserve their meat. They believe frog meat has medicinal values. It's given to new mothers.'

'They taste like chicken,' I replied.

'Oh, so you've have eaten them?'

'How do you think Nakul and I survived in the jungles after our home was bombed?'

'You're very strong, Indira. I feel sad thinking of you and your brother going through so much,' said Emily.

'We weren't the only ones. There are so many children like us who are still trying their best to survive. Think of them when you're scared of getting those frogs. It's the least we can do.' I squeezed her shoulder. 'Come on, let's go.'

'Right now? It's evening,' Emily said.

'Frogs are hunted at night. We may not find as many during the day,' I suggested.

'What if there are snakes? I hope you know snakes live off frogs. They may be out there hunting like us,' she joked.

'That just means we may have competition,' I laughed.

'It could be dangerous. I'm ready to die for a free India, but not to die from a snake bite on a silly frog hunt,' she said.

'We don't have to be killed by a bullet to be called patriotic, Emily,' I said. 'I'm ready to give up my life in any manner, as long as it's towards bringing freedom to our motherland. I don't care if it's a snake bite, a fall, or being trampled by an elephant. I just want to be on duty when it happens.'

Emily was out of reasons. 'All right, let's go. But can we be careful? Imagine people saying Rani Indira, the youngest warrior of Netaji's army, died while catching a frog.' Emily and I laughed.

'Rani Rosamma, the frog-slayer, the defender of the nation,' I teased, imitating a deep voice. We laughed until our stomachs hurt. We had had enough of forest treks.

We no longer found them as amusing as we found them initially when we left the camp.

'Don't you think we are seasoned soldiers now, with so much of walking over the days. Well, soldiers who fight on foot are called infantry. Male soldiers are referred as infantry-men. What do you think we are, infantry-women?' she joked. 'And you, Indira, infantry-child?' she laughed again.

'Do you think people will talk about our bravery?' I asked her. 'Do you think stories about our spying will be told to children?'

'Why not?' she said. 'When we march into India, people will gather along the streets and gape at the Ranis in awe. We'll be known as the avatars of Rani Lakshmi Bai of Jhansi and Goddess Durga.'

'What if we're forgotten about when history is written? What if nobody remembers us?'

She thought about this for a second. 'I won't lie. That *could* happen. The INA has thousands of soldiers. It's quite possible we won't be remembered individually. But then, we're not just Emily, Indira or even Laxmi. We're the Rani of Jhansi Regiment. The day we put on our uniform, we shed our egos and became part of this force that's greater than us all.'

Emily was right. 'When I joined the regiment, I didn't think of glory. My only thought was to free India,' I said.

By now, we'd reached the pond. I looked around. Green frog, black frog, grey frog, brown frog—but no yellow frog. Some were near the bushes, some near the banks, some sitting on rocks at the edge and some in the middle of the pond.

'Where are the bright yellow ones we saw the other day?' Emily asked.

I made a guess: 'They're here. These are the same ones. They turn yellow during the first rain.'

'Are you sure they're frogs and not some distant cousins of chameleons?'

'Silly you. These are frogs. See, no tail.' I quickly grabbed one and showed her. The frog wriggled to escape. Emily opened the earthen pot, and I dropped the frog in it and she briskly covered the mouth with a lid.

'Let's walk ahead,' I said.

Emily looked scared. 'More in the slush? There could be snakes.'

'I know, but frogs and snakes are food for humans. Didn't we learn to catch snakes and eat them in our jungle survival training?' I asked.

'We did. They tasted like fish.'

'Here's one big bull frog.' I slowly stepped closer and was about to catch it, when it jumped on Emily. The pot went flying from her hands and she fell in the knee-deep water with a huge splash.

'Ooh, what a fall!' I couldn't help laughing. 'Look, you were avoiding the slush and now you're covered in it.'

'Don't be so full of glee,' she snapped. 'Check if the frog in the pot has escaped.'

The pot was floating in the water without a scratch on it, but the frog had leaped away.

'Oh no! We have to do it all over again now,' I cried.

'It was just one frog. We were at the beginning of this frog-catching mission. Now, since I'm already covered in mud, I don't mind getting in with you. Though I'm still not sure this frog-selling idea will get us closer to the British officers,' she said.

The two of us got to work, catching a total of twenty-one frogs. They jumped around in the pot so much that it became difficult to keep the lid on, so we tied my scarf over it to hold it in place.

We didn't get much sleep that night, constantly waking up to the grunting sounds of the frogs. I felt sorry for them, but I couldn't free them. After all, they were our ticket into a British officer's residence, though I was starting to grow worried because of Emily's doubts. Only the next day would reveal if my frog plan was foolproof or total foolishness.

Chapter 24

EARS TO THE GROUND

'Grr ... groo ... croo ...' The frogs weren't any quieter the next morning.

'They're attracting too much attention, Indira,' commented Emily.

'Shh, shh,' I said, looking down at the pot. 'See, I tried. They aren't listening to me.'

'I just hope nobody gets suspicious,' she said.

'Don't worry. We're following a British officer's order. Nobody will dare stop us,' I said.

On reaching the house, I was hoping the colonel would come out and check the frogs himself. Instead, only the batman looked at them. If I couldn't speak to the officer, all our efforts would be wasted.

'Will saheb not check them personally,' I asked.

He laughed. 'I do that for him. He has more important work. The war is at our doorstep.'

'What next,' Emily whispered into my ear.

'You're an important man too. You shouldn't dirty your hands with unclean frogs. Your job is to give instructions. We'll clean and cook them,' I suggested.

'I won't pay you anything more. I'll just pay you for the frogs. That's it,' he said.

I smiled. 'You have a deal.'

He led us into the kitchen through a narrow back door, which was meant only for workers. 'Let me see how you clean and cut them,' he said, standing behind us and looking over our shoulders.

One thing I've noticed about frogs is that each one has a different personality. Some of the frogs in the pot had given up and submitted to their fate. Some weakly croaked. But one, right at the mouth of the pot, was trying to leap out. I closed the lid quickly. Then I opened it again. The frog was ready to jump out. I closed it again.

'Stop fooling around!' the batman shouted.

I opened the lid. The lively frog leaped out of the pot. It sat still, but its skin moved up and down with its breathing. It seemed like it looked at me accusingly and then leaped out of the kitchen into the corridor. It leaped ahead, and again sat still in the corridor outside two doors facing each other.

'Catch it. Catch it. Direct it into a room, and trap it there,' he ordered.

'The frog doesn't follow commands,' Emily who was following him shot back. It leaped ahead, and got a long leap to land straight in the parlour.

'Oh no! Catch it!' he yelled, and I went after it.

'Saheb shouldn't see the frog outside the kitchen. Otherwise, he'll eat you, not the frogs,' he warned.

'Let me handle this,' I said. The frog was hiding under a chair. I knelt down and stretched out my hand, but it didn't move. I wanted it to escape and leap around the house, so that I could get to go around the house on the pretext of catching the frog. I was reluctant to catch it, when it jumped into the corridor and then the parlour, to hide under the mantel. We were at the end of the corridor that opened into the parlour.

'I told you saheb shouldn't see this chaos,' the batman hissed through clenched teeth.

The batman's saheb and another man, an officer, I guessed, were sitting with their backs to us, discussing something.

'Quickly,' the batman instructed.

'I told you not to hurry me. If I make one wrong move, the frog will land straight on your saheb's bald head,' I whispered. I deliberately moved slower and waited longer, eavesdropping on the conversation.

'13 March, you say?' asked the officer.

'Yes, it's from a reliable source. The Japanese have planned an attack on the 13th. We need to be prepared with our defences and reinforcements,' the other man said.

'Quick!' muttered the batman.

I put my hand under the mantel hoping the frog would escape again and give me a little longer to eavesdrop, but the frog jumped and a porcelain showpiece fell and shattered.

'Who's that?' The officers turned.

'Nobody, sir! Just the errand girl cleaning,' the batman said.

'Don't pay her. This is for the loss of the showpiece,' he ordered and returned to his smoke and chatter.

I caught the frog and returned to the kitchen. As I prepared the frog meat, I wondered how I could keep coming to the house.

'We could cook this too. Shall we?' I asked.

The batman was fanning himself, sweating in the humid weather. He must have been feeling lazy because he said, 'Go ahead.' Then he added, 'You need to clean the places the frog landed on.'

'Why should I?' I said, pretending to be irritated.

'That's your punishment,' he said.

Emily and I cooked and then swept and mopped the entire house, but could not gather any more inputs.

'Is this house never cleaned? Emily asked. 'There's so much dust in the corners and under the furniture.'

The batman smirked. 'Why don't you come clean it every day?'

'We could, if you pay us. We're looking for work,' Emily said.

'We've had enough of frogs and snails. We need money to buy food,' I said.

'I like snail meat, though,' he replied.

'We don't work for free,' Emily declared.

'I'll pay you in food, not money,' he said. We'd found our way in.

That evening, I told Bishnu Da what I had overheard.

'13 March, eh?' he said, looking a little worried.

'What's happening on 13 March?' I asked.

'Looks like the British have placed moles among our men,' he replied.

'One of the officers also mentioned something about the Japanese attacking on the 13th. Is that so?' I asked.

Bishnu Da didn't reply. 'The 13th is just a fortnight away. We have so little time,' he said.

'How can we help?' Emily asked.

'Get more intel. Maybe get hold of a map of their deployment—asap.'

We'd seen the entire house while cleaning. There were no maps or plans lying around unattended. We had to get into the offices. This wasn't going to be easy.

Emily and I devised a plan.

At dawn, we went into the paddy fields and collected some snails, and were lucky to get some eels too. We entered the camp again with the earthen pot, pretending to have brought the officer our latest wares.

'I noticed you mentioned snail meat yesterday. I got this just for you,' Emily said to the batman while I was feeding the horses. 'May I cook it for you?' she asked.

'Sure, but don't think I'm going to give you any money,' he said.

'Just some more work and some food in return will do. Finding work in the village is not easy,' she replied. More work meant spending longer hours at the Saheb's house, and more access.

By the end of the day, we were nowhere closer to the offices and had no new information. Our plan had not worked. He didn't divulge any secrets despite her sweet talk or gift of snail meat. We didn't lose hope. We had learnt in our classes that to gather input, we need to be patient. It takes time to win trust and cultivate a source. Being too enthusiastic or trying to get inputs in a short time could lead to suspicion and failure. So, we continued working diligently for a couple of more days.

One evening, the rest of the staff busied themselves preparing a special dinner for a visitor.

'Who's coming today?' I asked the driver.

'Some friend of the saheb from the Royal Air Force,' he said.

'There are planes here too? The ones that go around dropping bombs?' I asked. He didn't reply. 'My younger brother says these planes poop. For a long time, he didn't know they were bombs.'

At that, he burst into laughter. 'Poop! That's really something. I say my motor car is better than a plane any day.'

'Your car cannot fly. An airplane soars like a bird. Whoever flies one must be very skilled,' I said.

'What do you mean "very skilled"? We drivers need to be more skilled. We drive through rough roads, hilly terrain, deserts—we even cross rivers. A plane cannot take off without an airstrip. Anyone can fly an airplane on an unobstructive sky or drive a vehicle on a clean clear road. The real challenge is driving a vehicle through obstacles,' he said.

'Planes could be shot down, isn't it?' I said.

'So could we. Anyone could shoot us or bomb us. Enemies can even simply toss a hand grenade at us,' he said.

'Is there that thing here in Tedim? That thing they need to first run the plane on?' I asked.

'You mean an airstrip? No, no. Unlike cars, planes can't be parked anywhere. Kakching has one of the two all-weather airstrips in this region. That's where Saheb's friend has come from,' the driver said.

'What's all-weather? Do they have seasons?'

'All-weather means there's no issue after a bout of rain. No slush. No dirt. Solid tarred road. The airplane can still take off after a night of rain.'

'Where's the other all-weather airstrip?' I asked.

'Why do you need so many details?' he snapped.

I shrugged. 'Just like that. I've never seen a plane up close. What you're saying is so interesting that I thought I could share it with my brother,' I said.

'Your brother? Isn't it just you and your sister who survived and are finding your way back?' he asked.

I'd slipped up. 'I mean my brother who is lost. We don't know where he went. Maybe when I find my brother, I'll tell him all the things I learnt from you.' I wept loudly.

'Shh! Stop crying,' he said. 'This is why sahebs should never employ girls, and that too kids. Shut up now.'

'I miss my brother! I miss my parents!' I cried.

'Come on, shut your mouth and wipe your tears,' he said. 'I miss my family too, okay? I haven't heard from them. They have no news of me. They probably think I'm lost. Perhaps your brother is somewhere safe like me.'

I continued to cry but sputtered, 'Y-you r-remind me of Baba. He used to tell me stories. Th-thank y-you for telling me about planes. I wish girls could drive!' I cried harder.

'They do, they do!' he said quickly. He was desperate to get me to shut up. 'Princess Elizabeth, who will become the queen of England after her father's time as king, is a military driver like me,' he said proudly.

'Really? The princess too? That means you have a royal job.'

He laughed. 'Yes, I suppose I'm like a raja.'

'Do you drive anything apart from motor cars?' I asked.

'I drive huuuge trucks too,' he boasted.

'Any army trucks?'

'I sat in a tank once! The earth trembles under it when it rolls ahead. It crushes everything under it.'

'Do they have tanks here?'

'They're usually used in the plains, but history could be made here. There was a test run with M3 tanks on hills for the first time. That's when I sat in one. Imagine the scene when a tank rolls over the hilltops and takes down the Japanese,' he said.

Emily and I waited for Bishnu Da that night. We had both collected some strategic information.

My notes read: *Kakching one of two all-weather airstrips of the Allied Forces. Medium M3 tanks could be used against the INA and Japanese.*

'Excellent, Indira. You've confirmed some of our earlier inputs. The Gandhi Brigade will attack the Pallel base from the north along with the Japanese, and also take control of the Kakching airstrip,' he said.

'What do you think of the M3 tanks?' I asked.

'We'll need more information. M3s haven't been used in mountainous regions and in tropical jungles so far. They have been used in North Africa. I don't think they can take the ups and downs of these steep hills and thick jungles,' Bishnu Da said.

'But the driver said he sat in one. There was a trial.'

'He must have been fantasising,' he said.

'Is the INA prepared? Do we have tanks?' I asked.

'We don't. The Japanese have Ha-Go tanks. They were successfully used by the Japanese to defeat the British and take over Malaya and Singapore. They've proven brilliant in these thick jungles,' he said.

'Have the Ha-Gos ever faced M3s?'

'The British don't believe tanks are suitable for jungle warfare. They never had any tanks in these regions,' he said.

'Please check. Don't dismiss my input,' I pleaded.

'I promise you, I'll deliver all your inputs, regardless of what I think of the information. The analysis is done by senior officers,' he replied.

Emily lit a fire and eagerly waited for me to finish while she boiled some eggs. She was excited to share what she had uncovered. 'At various points, there are artillery units. They consist of two batteries: one of field artillery and one of mountain artillery,' she said.

'Go on,' said Bishnu Da.

I was curious. 'What's the difference between field and mountain artillery?' I asked.

Bishnu Da answered my question. 'Basically, field artillery guns are mobile and can be moved around easily to support the infantry. Mountain artillery can be fired from behind and over a mountain. Continue, Emily Rosamma.'

She smiled. 'Well, the field artillery unit is full of British soldiers and the mountain artillery battery is made up of Indian soldiers.'

'Excellent,' said Bishnu Da. 'We need to turn the Indian soldiers against the British. Then, when the INA marches, the Indian soldiers won't attack us but will join us.'

'Will they?' I asked.

'Netaji firmly believes that every Indian is seeking freedom. When the INA marches to victory, the Indian soldiers in the British Army may join us in our fight for freedom,' he said.

'What if they don't join us but continue to attack the INA forces?' I asked.

'Well, we need to prepare for that too. We need the specific locations of these artillery regiments and all other units. Then our forces will be aware of what to expect ahead and can be prepared to retaliate. We need a map with all the locations of their troops marked,' he said.

'We didn't see one anywhere in the house,' said Emily.

'It must be in the office. It'll *definitely* be in what they call the operations room, or ops room. You two need to break into it.'

'That's not easy. They don't let us anywhere close to the office,' said Emily.

'Find a way. You must have noted their routine by now. See how you can sneak in.'

I had an idea. 'The offices are cleaned by the soldiers on housekeeping duty. I've seen two of them going towards the offices in the morning, between 7.30 and 8 a.m., after breakfast but before the office opens. Their routine is similar to what we followed at the INA camp,' I said.

'So, what's your plan?' asked Emily.

'After physical training in the mornings, most of the soldiers are in the mess until 7.30 a.m. We could go between 7 and 7.30 a.m., disguised as Indian soldiers going to sweep and mop the office.'

Bishnu Da clapped. 'Brilliant!'

'We'll need disguises,' said Emily.

Bishnu Da rummaged around in his dirty gunny sack. He pulled out two pairs of khaki shorts and white shirts. 'Will these do?' he asked.

'They should,' replied Emily, sniffing the clothes and pulling a face.

'Well, soldiers,' he said, 'time to go get us that map.'

Chapter 25

EYES ALL AROUND

Mornings are kind of funny, aren't they? It's when people are technically the most awake but are the least alert. We wake up with a list of chores we have to do during the day. In the first couple of hours, we behave as though we'll finish everything before noon. Then, as the sun rises higher, slip into our lazy selves.

We entered the camp as usual with our wares. 'How come so early today? It's not yet time for civilian entry,' said the guard.

'Saheb ordered us to get some quail eggs for his breakfast. He'll be furious if we're late,' I said, getting us in without more trouble.

We quickly ducked behind a thicket. We pulled off our wrap-around skirts and wrapped turbans around our heads to hide our hair.

'How do I look?' I asked.

'Like a sweet young boy,' said Emily. 'And me?'

'Handsome,' I replied.

We uncovered our baskets to pull out a steel bucket,

a broom and a mopping cloth. Chins up and standing straight, we felt taller than we were.

'Remember what we learnt about disguises?' asked Emily.

'If you doubt yourself, others definitely will. Confidence is the best disguise,' I said.

'When you lie, lie confidently. You should believe your lie. If not, no one else will,' she added.

'And most important ...'

'Never get caught,' we said together.

We walked past the soldiers rushing to the bathrooms, finishing their mugs of tea, immersed in thought, polishing their boots, shining the brass on their uniforms and humming songs. The morning routine was on, and everyone was lost in their own little world. A little later, they would all suddenly snap back to reality and hurry to get to their duties.

At the office, the atmosphere was sleepier—but we got a rude shock. The rooms weren't open. The office had a long verandah with high arches on one side and there were several rooms in line on the other side looking over the garden across the verandah. The heavy wooden doors of these rooms had huge locks. The locks were wrapped with a cloth, which was sealed over with melted wax, and an insignia of the military division was stamped over it with a wax steal stamp.

'What now?' I whispered to Emily.

'We just have to wait. I guess they follow a protocol to open the doors,' she whispered back.

'When do you think that will happen?'

'Someone assigned to the task will come and unseal the locks, and then key them open, I think.'

'Maybe they do it to make sure no one enters the offices after they've left for the night. A tampered seal shows that someone might have broken in or tried to,' I said.

'Oh, why didn't we think of this earlier?' said Emily. 'Why didn't we notice anything like this at the INA offices?'

'It's not our fault. The main strategy offices weren't at the Rani camp. We never went to the INA side during non-office hours.' I wanted to make Emily feel better, but I was worried about what a huge mistake this was.

'We weren't prepared for this,' said Emily.

'Yes, that's what makes fieldwork more challenging,' I said.

'You know what? We need to improvise,' she declared.

We swept the deserted corridors to avoid anyone questioning us. That also gave us enough time to read the boards on all doors and find the ops room, where we hoped we could find something important. The huge round clock with black rim and white dial, hung at the end of the corridor facing the entrance showed the time to be 7.25 a.m., when we heard heavy footsteps and the clanging of keys.

'Should we hide?' I asked.

'No. We belong here, remember? Act like it.'

A group of four walked by us while we continued to sweep. They opened the seals and unlocked the doors. Then one of them turned towards me and ordered, 'Finish the operations room first. We need it soon,' and proceeded to the other offices. We walked to the ops room, which was third from the end, among the several rooms in line.

Emily and I quickly entered the room and looked around. There was a desk and few chairs around it on one side. A sand model was placed in the middle of the room showing the terrain, the attack and defence plans, and where the British forces were positioned. A map on the wall showed us the same things. I pulled out the sheet of paper I'd carried and started to sketch everything as fast as I could.

'Make sure to note down the signs correctly,' said Emily. She'd been sweeping the doorstep for the last few minutes to keep anyone from entering.

I tried to remember everything I'd learnt in my map reading classes. There were so many signs and symbols—a ring with one dot, a ring with three dots, a ring with a single line, a ring with two lines—for sections, platoons, companies and battalions. I noted down the positions of the infantry, artillery, ammunition dumps and airstrips. I drew arrows showing attack plans and marked routes, rivers, bridges and passes.

'Quickly! Somebody might come,' hurried Emily.

I continued drawing, my hands shaking now.

'Are you done? Quick!' Emily whispered.

'You constantly asking me if I'm done won't make it go faster! Let me concentrate,' I shot back.

'Okay, okay! I'm just worried that the real housekeeping staff might come soon and find us here.'

'Almost there,' I said as I cross-checked the map with the sand model and my drawings. Then I looked through the desk and the dust bin.

'Check the fireplace. All classified documents are usually burnt,' said Emily. 'And be quick,' she couldn't help but add.

'I found something. Most of the page is burnt but there's a heading: Op Thursday.'

'Today is Thursday. If there's nothing else, we should get going,' Emily said. This time, I agreed. We walked quickly towards the exit—and spotted the real housekeepers walking towards us. We took a sharp right. When we reached the end of the corridor, we heard someone call, 'Hey! Hey! Stop! Who are you?' We continued walking briskly. 'Stop them!' someone yelled.

'Should we run?' I whispered.

'No, that'll make them more suspicious. Let's face them while there's some distance between us,' Emily said. We turned. 'What is it? Why are you yelling?' she screamed back in a hoarse voice.

'Who sent you here?' the soldier yelled back.

'You first tell me why you were so late. Saheb was furious and we were summoned. We have no interest in doing someone else's thankless job. Subedar is waiting for you,' she shot back. The men hurried inside.

'Well done! You totally fooled them,' I said.

'Now, walk confidently until we leave the building and reach the turn with the thick trees. Then, run.'

The best part about military camps in those regions was that they were full of patches of dense forest. The trees inside the camp gave us easy spots to hide out. During our visits through the weeks, Emily and I had noted several entry and exit points, some official, some unofficial, some through the fence and some over the fence.

The office complex was behind high walls. I had made a mental note of that before entering.

'Come, climb this tree,' I told Emily.

'Are you out of your mind, Indira? I know you love doing it, but we can't keep sitting up in trees. We need to find a way out,' she said.

'This is the way.' I smiled and climbed the crooked mango tree. 'Follow me,' I called out. Emily looked unsure at first, but then began climbing. I slowly crawled along the branch that went across the compound wall and towards the other side. Emily was close behind me.

'How do we get down now?' she asked.

I untied the turban on my head, tied one end of it to the branch and let the other end down. 'Now's the time to use our rope-climbing training,' I said and slithered down. We were out, back in the jungle.

Bishnu Da had been waiting for us. Seeing him, we both screamed, 'Mission successful!'

'Let me be the one to decide that,' he said, though he grinned. 'I'm glad you're both safe. You clearly remembered the most important rule: never get caught.'

I was excited to show him the map I'd drawn. 'Fabulous,' he said, looking at it closely. 'You've got the details, but just explain your handwriting in some places. I can't follow what you've written.'

'I wish there was something we could use to just capture the look of plans and maps,' I said.

'You mean a camera. I saw an Englishman use it in Singapore. It's bulky and is easily noticeable,' said Emily.

'Perhaps they should get some small handy cameras for spies,' I said.

'I've never seen a small camera. The ones I've seen are like rectangular boxes,' she said.

Bishnu Da looked up from the maps. 'The Azad Hind Fauj may not have the budget for fancy gadgets for every agent, but it has dedicated, smart and patriotic soldiers. Devices can be bought, but courage and loyalty cannot.

That makes all the difference. You've both done an excellent job,' he said.

'So the map is of help, Bishnu Da?' I asked.

'Great help. I need to get this to the Subhas Brigade soon. They'll be crossing the Chindwin River any day now. They have a long way to march until Imphal. The Gandhi Brigade is marching from the east and will join them in Imphal. The Nehru and Azad Brigades will come in the next stage,' he said.

'What are our further orders?' Emily asked.

'You need to leave this place immediately. You might have left enough clues behind at the British camp for them to doubt you. They might already be out looking for you.'

'Yes. The baskets and clothes we left behind, the turban cloth hanging from the tree—there are definitely enough clues. We need to escape in disguise,' I said.

'Go towards Imphal. Cross the Manipur River and wait for me and other members of the Bahadur Group. We will find you,' Bishnu Da said. He led us to a narrow road in the jungle and we walked along it to a village hidden between two hills.

Bishnu Da had arranged a horse and some food for the journey. Emily and I sat on the one saddle and rode off. I remembered the first time I had seen Captain Lakshmi riding a horse. I had hoped I would do the same. There I was, living my dream, riding into India.

Chapter 26

BLOOD AND BRIDGE

I wish I could say that the horse ride was smooth, but it was anything but. It was a disbalancing, back-breaking, bone-crunching, muscle-twisting, exhausting ride. But was it adventurous? Oh yes. We were dodging danger constantly. We avoided the main roads and made our way through the jungle. Sometimes the twigs hit our faces, some branches almost knocked us off the horse. At one point, I was almost bitten by a green vine snake, hanging low from a branch, maybe waiting for a passer-by. Thankfully, I always remember Ma's instructions to Nakul and me when we stepped out to play: 'Keep your eyes open. Always look up as well as down. Watch your step for insects and snakes on the ground, and look up for the green vine snakes that can bite your heads.'

We had ridden for some days at that point, taking turns to be rider and pillion, stopping for water breaks and night halts. The few fruits and rice we were carrying were exhausted, and so was the horse. I cannot really call him a friendly horse. He seemed rather snobbish and looked angry. I felt like he was waiting for a chance to throw us off his back. I still don't know how Bishnu Da arranged the horse. Did he steal it from the British? Something that *had* been stolen from the British was a plane that the Japanese had taken, we later found out. The sounds of explosions at a distance startled the horse and perhaps made him distrust us.

Avoiding the villages and clueless about what was happening with the war, we simply continued finding our way through the jungle, heading towards the Manipur River. One evening, we were lucky enough to catch a pheasant for dinner. After feeding the horse, finding a water source and setting up camp, it was completely dark. I was exhausted. I just wanted to rest my head on a pillow and go to sleep, and so fumbled around trying to find some leaves to make a pile. Instead, I felt something soft, which felt like cloth. I rolled it up to use it as pillow and rested my head on it. I immediately fell asleep.

'Indira! Wake up!' It was Emily, shaking me awake the next morning.

'What?' I looked up at her, rubbing my eyes.

'What are you sleeping on? Just look at it,' she said.

It was a bundle of clothes. A blood-stained khaki uniform.

I ran to the side of the river and hurled my guts out.

An old woman, bent over her walking stick, had come to the river to fill water. 'This uniform must have belonged to someone whose family is waiting for him,' she said in a raspy voice. 'You've pushed it away, but there might be someone waiting to hold it dearly. They may never get to see their loved one again.'

'War is ugly. War is cruel,' Emily cried.

'It is, child. When we speak of war, we speak only of kings, generals and politicians. We don't speak of the many lives lost and the many families broken,' the woman said.

'I lost my parents to war. They weren't even soldiers. My brother and I lost our childhoods,' I said.

'What about you? Why are you here?' Emily asked the old woman.

'I'm waiting for death,' she replied.

Emily and I looked at her, confused. 'My family and the others all left the village because of the war. I'm too weak to walk far and didn't want to slow my children and grandchildren down. I wouldn't have survived the trek anyway. It's better to die in my homeland than a foreign land. So I chose to stay,' she said. 'What about you? Why are you here?'

'We lost our way. We're also escaping the war,' I said. We helped her carry water from the river back to her hut and continued our journey.

We didn't speak for a long time, until Emily finally broke the silence, saying, 'We're living in turbulent times. Though we're fighting for India's freedom, we're also fighting alongside the Japanese. So many countries are involved in this.'

'Like Bishnu Da keeps saying, we're fighting this war so that Indians no longer have to fight any wars for foreigners,' I said.

It was high time we got out of hiding in the jungles. The villages were deserted. Empty mortars shells lay strewn around, and homes lay burnt. The booming sound of explosions were heard on and off. We needed to cross the river to the other side soon.

'There was a bridge in the map we copied,' I remembered.

'Yes, the bridge across the Manipur River,' Emily said.

'We need to find it to get across.'

'Do you remember the map, Indira? Maybe you can remember a route from it.'

'Wait! I have the map,' I said.

'No you don't. I saw you hand it over to Bishnu Da.'

'I made a copy,' I said, pulling out a folded sheet of paper.

'Bishnu Da asked us not to keep anything that could get us caught,' she said, taking the sheet from me and unfolding it. She held it up. 'This is blank. There's nothing on it. This is no time for pranks!'

'Wait here a second,' I said and rushed into the kitchens of each of the abandoned houses. In one of them, there were embers in a dying fire in the kitchen. Perhaps, the houses were recently abandoned. I blew over the embers and lit a fire with some dry leaves. I held the paper over it at a distance, just enough for the sheet to get hot. Brown lines slowly began appearing on the paper. Soon, the whole map was on it.

'What is this!' Emily squealed in disbelief. 'How did you do this?'

'A trick I learnt from our friend Harpreet,' I replied. 'When at the village waiting for Bishnu Da, I plucked a lemon from the tree we were standing under. While you and Da went to get the horse and food, I squeezed out the lemon juice. I used a bird feather to draw the map.'

'Why did Harpreet use this trick?' Emily asked.

'Let's just say there was a certain INA soldier she was keen on writing to. Come on, the maps says we need to go this way.'

We rode alongside the Manipur River until we reached the bridge. It was full of people desperate to get across. There was total chaos—mothers clinging to their babies and walking under the weight of their belongings, fathers trying to find a cart or any vehicle to ferry their children, men herding cattle that could help feed their families, old people trying to keep up with their children and grandchildren. Everyone was trying to leave the land their forefathers had built their homes on.

'The war has come. Let's leave before it catches us,' said a father to his little son.

'It's almost here. Hurry,' said an old woman to her friend.

I looked at Emily. 'It seems like the battle has started,' she said.

We walked with the horse onto the narrow bridge, jostling for space until we reached the end.

'Bishnu Da asked us to meet him and other Bahadur members here. So where exactly do we go?' I asked Emily.

'I'm not sure. At least we've crossed the river. I think we need to take shelter for now.'

The villagers walked down a path in the valley. We waited for a few minutes, wondering if we should follow them or take another route.

'I think we should wait. Let's climb up the hill and camp out,' I suggested.

'Yes, that'll give us a better view of the grounds below,' Emily said.

From up on the hill, we watched people flee their homeland. She didn't say anything, but I was sure Emily was thinking about the same thing I was: the number of victims war takes.

After sunset, we started hearing all kinds of noises: heavy footsteps, the creaking of wheels, horse hooves, the loud rumble of engines. We tried looking down, but we could see very little in the dark. Then, suddenly, a huge explosion lit up the sky—the bridge was up in flames. In its light, we could see British Indian soldiers on our side of the riverbank.

'The British are retreating. The Subhas Brigade and the Japanese Imperial Army must be close,' said Emily.

'And they must have put up a tough fight. That's why the British Army has burnt the bridge—to stop them from crossing over,' I said.

'Well, if I've understood their strategy, their next move will be to occupy the heights. They will position themselves on hills and will attack our forces when they get closer,' guessed Emily.

'We need to leave now then,' I said, turning to where we'd left the horse—but there was no horse. 'Oh! It must have bolted after the explosion,' I said. We began making our way down. We walked all night, keeping away from the makeshift British camp, and stopped only when we reached an abandoned village. Maybe it was the noise of us breaking a door open or of the dogs that barked at us, but something must have alerted the people in the village. We were suddenly surrounded by men and women pointing guns at us. Shocked, we raised our hands and looked around, wondering what our next move should be. Just as I was thinking of an escape plan, there was a loud cackle of laughter.

'It's you two! You managed not to get caught until now,' said Bishnu Da. It took us a couple of seconds to recognise him in the torchlight. He was no longer a beggar. Clean shaven and hair well combed, wearing a smart kurta and dhoti, he looked dapper.

'Meet some of the other members of the Bahadur Group,' he said. There were two Ranis disguised as dancers, wearing long flowing skirts, glittering blouses, fine dupattas and matching jewellery. They would dance to entertain villagers at village fairs and also perform for soldiers at events organised in their stations. Three others were dressed as boys. The men were dressed as hunters, boatmen, even British Army soldiers.

'They have all been in the field like you, collecting and passing on intel,' Bishnu Da said. 'In fact, Haneef and Bhairav'—he pointed out the one dressed like a British soldier—'used your intel and sabotaged an enemy asset.'

'What do you mean?' I asked.

'Looking at the map you brought us, we could locate the ammunition depot of the British. Bhairav and Haneef entered the premises and lit a spark, which blew up all the ammunition.'

'Bravo! Where is the other soldier, Haneef?' asked Emily.

'He couldn't make it out in time. He sacrificed himself,' Bhairav said. He hung his head.

To break the silence, I said, 'We saw the British forces retreating. They seem really scared of the Subhas Brigade.'

'Yes, we've gained some ground. Instead of 13 March, the INA and the Japanese crossed the Chindwin and launched a surprise attack on 8 March,' Bishnu Da said.

'Could they have advanced their date of attack because they knew that the British were preparing for the 13th?' asked Emily.

'Your intel must have helped make the decision, Rosamma. I don't know. I'm just a courier. Those decisions are taken by senior officers,' he said.

'As you said, the army works as a team. We've all contributed,' said Emily.

Bishnu Da nodded. 'Yes, some Bahadur Group members have acted as pathfinders and are fighting alongside the Subhas Brigade. Madhu and Manisha, disguised as dancers, got us intel about Op Thursday.'

'Yes,' I interrupted, 'we saw a burnt document with 'Op Thursday' written on it. We didn't know what it meant. Since the document was burnt and I couldn't retrieve anything, we didn't think much of it.'

'The British and Americans launched Operation Thursday on 5 March. They sent airborne fighters into northern Burma. We couldn't stop it, but we were at least prepared. That helped a great deal,' he said.

'So what's the next plan of action for us?' Emily asked.

'The Subhas Brigade is leading the attack from the south and the Gandhi Brigade is entering from the east. While the British troops are busy engaged on these two fronts, the rest of the Bahadur Group has stealthily made its way northwards towards Imphal,' Bishnu Da said.

'Oh really! I thought we were only providing intel and acting as spies and pathfinders,' said Madhu.

'We also fight on the front when the need arises,' replied Bhairav.

'At first light, we will march ahead to join the Bahadur Group at their hideout,' ordered Bishnu Da.

Chapter 27

JAI HIND!

I sometimes wondered if Bishnu Da was a magician. We hardly knew anything about him, but he seemed to know everything. How else did he always know how to find us? Whenever we had questions, he'd have the answers. And the gunny sack he carried was like a magician's top hat. Whatever we needed, he'd just reach in and pull it out. The next morning, when we reported to leave, we saw that he'd somehow arranged for a donkey to carry some of the load. I still don't know how he did it.

After a long trek over hills, streams and fields, getting closer to our destination, Bishnu Da once again pulled out random things from the load the donkey was carrying: uniforms of different sizes, shoes, ammunition and rifles stolen from the British. While we changed into the uniforms, Bishnu Da scribbled something in his diary. He left it on a rock and went along with Bhairav. Unable to resist, I quickly flipped through the pages.

The entries were similar—just a few words and the date the entry was made. The last entry read:

13 April 1944
Hot, humid day.
Light rain at 4 a.m.
Marched to Bahadur camp.

The other pages had similar entries. Some seemed silly, like the one where he'd written about our squabble over not having got the map: *Argument with agents Rani Indira and Rani Rosamma.*

There were some other entries about the villages nearby: *Cases of malaria reported in village. Bout of dysentery in village. Villagers drank water from pond next to elephant rock.*

Some days, he simply mentioned food and the weather: *Heavy rain last night. Ate mushrooms and ferns.*

While I was busy reading, Bishnu Da said over my shoulder, 'It's my digest. Tried to write something like the Digest of Service maintained in battalions. I wanted to have a record of the soldiers I oversaw and places I lived in. This information also helps us to recreate scenes from the past in case of any investigation. Some of these observations have helped our forces while marching ahead.' I turned around and saw him in uniform for the first time. That's when I realised he was not just our 'da', our brother, even though we treated him like one. He was our senior, Subedar Bishnu Kumar. We saluted him and waited for his orders to march ahead.

The camp site of the rear party of the Bahadur Group was buzzing with excitement and anticipation. A unit of the Japanese Imperial Army were camping along with us.

'We're going to take the British Army by surprise and shock them,' said Ustad Baldev Singh. Emily and I were glad to meet our instructor again.

'So, they aren't prepared?' Emily asked.

'Not at all. They don't expect an attack by the Azad Hind Fauj on this axis. Not in their wildest of dreams.' He chuckled.

'They might have been following the movement of the Subhas Brigade,' I suggested.

'Yes, they're expecting the Japanese. They underestimate us. Remember what I taught you in class: Never underestimate. Always be prepared.' He patted himself on the back. 'While the British were planning to avert an attack by the Subhas Brigade and the Gandhi Brigade, the Bahadur Group has silently advanced deep into Manipur. All their focus is on the road to Imphal. We are going to shock them.'

Soon after, we were all asked to stand in line for a briefing session. The commander of the Bahadur Group, Colonel Shaukat Ali Malik, was to address us. I was glad to be seeing him again, after we left the camp.

'What do you think this is about?' I asked.

'The next course of action, I guess,' Emily said.

'Will the Japanese be leading the attack?'

'Netaji wants the first drop of blood on Indian soil to be that of a soldier of the INA. He's ordered the officers to ensure that, and has given strict instructions that the INA will charge ahead,' she said. While Colonel Malik commanded the Bahadur Group, the Gandhi Brigade was commanded by Major General Mohammed Zaman Kiani, the Subhas Brigade by Major General Shah Nawaz Khan and the Azad Brigade by Colonel Gulzara Singh.

All of us looked up to them, trusting they would lead us to victory.

Colonel Malik walked in. 'Do you think he'll congratulate us?' I asked Emily.

'We've all worked hard. I don't think there's time to thank everyone individually,' she replied.

'That's true,' I said. 'Like Bishnu Da would say, the army works together. There are no individual victories.'

Colonel Malik began his address with a booming 'Jai Hind!' Everyone stood at attention, hanging on to every word he said next. 'Netaji and all of us are extremely proud of the Bahadur Group. We have successfully accomplished the missions assigned to us and have created history in espionage and sabotage. Our work helped the Subhas and Gandhi Brigades force the British to retreat from many of their strongholds. It was the intelligence provided by our agents that helped these groups plan and execute the attacks. The Nehru Brigade and the Azad Brigade are also waiting to launch their operations. And now, we're going to prove our combat capabilities.'

He pointed to a sand model, the kind we had seen in the British ops room. I wished I could turn and look at Emily, but we were all still standing at attention.

'After last light, we will march to Tronglaobi and attack the British Army base there in a phased manner and from three directions. Your respective platoon commanders will explain your roles to you.'

He pointed to the sand model again. 'Here's the broad battle plan. The first team will attack the main entrance, where there will be the most resistance from the armed guards. Once they secure the main entrance, the second team will attack from the west. After the west side is secure, the third team will attack from the east. Any questions?'

Ustad Baldev asked, 'What if we attacked from all directions at once? Wouldn't that be more impactful?'

'It would indeed. Here, our target is a small garrison. The field is not large. In this case, if we attack together from all directions, there's a risk we could harm each other while firing. Hence the phased attack,' Colonel Malik explained.

Bishnu Da spoke up. 'What about the fourth side—the north side? Isn't it better to encircle the garrison and attack from all four sides?'

Surrounding the enemy from all four sides seemed smarter. Colonel Malik seemed to have sensed our thoughts because he went on to explain. 'See, if the enemy feels that there is no escape, they'll fight back harder. But when the battle gets intense and they sense defeat, and there's an option to retreat, they'll choose to retreat. We'll leave the back open for them to escape. After all, the British Army also has our Indian brothers. Netaji hopes they'll lay down their arms and join the INA, rather than be killed for the British crown that doesn't care for them,' he explained. After a long pause to let his instructions sink in, he added, 'We need to stay focussed on our objective. See you all in the evening. Jai Hind.'

That evening, we marched to Tronglaobi. The British had retreated and abandoned all their garrisons except for this one. Divided in platoons, we dispersed in our groups and took our positions in different directions as instructed, around the hill on which the garrison that was to be attacked was. The sun had set and it was pitch dark. Some scouts who had done a recce of the routes led the platoons along with the experienced soldiers. Emily and I were in the last rows of the last group. Almost at the end. We followed the rest and climbed up stealthily in the dark.

'Can you see anything, Emily?' I whispered.

'No. Just follow the soldier ahead of you,' she whispered back.

'I know. And we're going to stay in a buddy pair, right?' I said.

'Of course, the same way we did these past months,' she said.

'I can't think of anyone else as my buddy. You've been the best.'

'I'm lucky to have served with you, Rani Indira Laxmi. I want to tell you that in case this is our last mission.'

'Oh, don't say that! We're not going to die. Remember our mantra of 'do not get caught'? The same applies here: do not get killed.'

'But when we go to battle, we should be ready to die. Netaji said, "Give me blood and I shall give you freedom."'

'We'll give him blood tonight, just not ours.'

Emily giggled. 'You're quite confident before your first battle.'

'Just like aiming for a mango with a stone, it's about your belief. If you believe you'll miss the mango, you'll definitely miss. If you believe you're going to eat that mango, you'll hit it. I believe I'm going to see the sunrise from the hilltop tomorrow,' I replied.

Just then, we heard the deafening sound of an explosion, and a cheer of 'Inquilab Zindabad!' The first team had stormed through the main gates. Bullets flew and then ... silence. The sky lit up with a red flare, quickly followed by a green flare. That was the signal. The first team had captured the post. The second team immediately attacked from the left. Shouts, gunshots, more explosions, and fire—the chaos was scary. Two more flares shot up. It was now the third team's turn to move.

We crawled through trenches and under fences. A grenade fell, exploding right ahead of us. We hit the ground. The battle felt so intense. From far away, it was all about the sounds of blasts and the glow of fires. But up close, those same sounds and sights turned monstrous, making you either super bold or super careful. I don't know what got into me, but I found myself running towards the fire.

There was another explosion. I turned around and saw Emily go down. I rushed towards her. A piece of shrapnel grazed her arm, narrowly missing her heart. Another had pierced her ankle. I quickly grabbed her and pushed her to the ground, while bullets went flying over our heads. Soon, the gunfire died down, and there were loud cheers of 'Bharat Mata ki jai!' We had captured our target. Supporting Emily, who was able to hobble, we made our way to the camp.

The grounds were lit under the full moon's glow. Some Indian soldiers of the British Army had surrendered and pledged to join the Indian National Army. The others had escaped from the back, the side that had been left open. Colonel Malik was right. We had taken them by shock and surprise. They hadn't expected our small Bahadur Group to have our strength. Most of the soldiers had been sleeping and their weapons were in the armoury when we attacked. Only the guards on duty and a few alert soldiers put up a fight, but they gave up when they realised how unprepared they were.

The full moon marked Cheiraoba, the new year for Manipuris. It was a new beginning for the Azad Hind Fauj too. We had been the first to successfully free a region in India from the British. We had created history. I had done my bit to get freedom for my motherland, India. And I had made Ma–Baba's wish come true: I was home—or very close to it.

Winning this battle meant so much more than just one army occupying land held by another. It was about gaining independence and moving towards self-rule. But it wouldn't mean much if the locals weren't on board. So, the next day, Colonel Malik met the village leaders and supporters of the INA.

'A good place to mark the change is Kangla, the holy seat of judgement and coronation of kings of the ancient Moirang kingdom,' suggested the village leader and freedom fighter Mairembam Koireng Singh.

'He's right. There's no better place symbolically. 14 April, the day of the Lunar New Year, is also auspicious,' said Naqi Ahmed Chaudhury, an INA soldier from Manipur who was Colonel Malik's interpreter.

At 5 p.m. on 14 April 1944, at Moirang Kangla, Colonel Shaukat Ali Malik became the first Indian to hoist the tricolour flag on Indian land freed from British control. The flag with the INA's springing tiger fluttered proudly against the backdrop of a saffron sky, white clouds and lush green hills.

'Today, you have all been freed from the clutches

of the British yoke. Many have died on our way here to Moirang, and many will die further on our march to Delhi. We will not rest until we free all of India and unfurl the tricolour at Lal Qila,' the colonel roared in his speech.

The flag had flown high in the Andaman and Nicobar Islands after the Japanese transferred control to the INA, but this was the first time the flag was flying on India's mainland. This victory had made us believe that we could defeat the British. But we still had a long way to go. Delhi was far. This was just the beginning.

'Inquilab Zindabad!' we all called out. 'Chalo Dilli.'

Jai Hind!

ACKNOWLEDGEMENTS

Perhaps I wouldn't have felt so strongly for Laxmi Panda if I hadn't heard her story in her own words. Hearing her recount her bravery made the story even more impactful for me. I'm forever grateful for her trust in sharing it with me. This encounter wouldn't have been possible without her grandson, Probin Raj Patro, who connected us in 2008. I thank Probin for his continued support while I wrote the book. He currently leads the Indira Laxmi Panda Memorial Trust.

Over the years, I lost touch with Laxmi's family. Finding them without an address or phone number seemed an uphill task. Thankfully, journalist and author Paresh Rath helped me reconnect with Probin. I appreciate his help.

I would also like to thank Anil Dhir, Convenor of

the INTACH Bhubaneshwar chapter. His research and evidence collection were instrumental in proving Laxmi Panda's claim as a member of the Rani of Jhansi Regiment. He arranged her meeting with then-President Pratibha Patil and secured her recognition with the Rashtriya Swatantrata Samman. Anil also documented her journey through articles, research papers and interviews, and she generously shared these with me during her final days in his care.

While the adventures in this book are fictional, the information and facts provided by these individuals were crucial in building the narrative.

Words cannot express the unwavering support I received from my husband, Sameer Srivastava and son, Abir. They were not only my biggest cheerleaders, pushing me to write, but also my first readers and fact-checkers. Sameer's military expertise proved invaluable in understanding tactics and military jargon. With his help, I could simplify WWII campaigns and weave them into the story around Laxmi.

I am grateful to my editor and publisher, Vidhi Bhargava, for believing in me once again. Despite missed deadlines, she remained patient and supportive. Vidhi and the Westland Books team has been very supportive with my debut book, *The Nameless God*. Their encouragement also propelled me to write this second book *Laxmi Panda: The Story of Netaji's Youngest Spy*. I thank them for taking Laxmi Panda's story to the world.

You May Also Like